Reaching and Teaching
DIVERSE
POPULATIONS

Reaching and Teaching
DIVERSE POPULATIONS
Strategies for Moving Beyond Stereotypes

MARY BELLUCCI BUCKELEW
West Chester University of Pennsylvania

ANDREA FISHMAN
West Chester University of Pennsylvania

Los Angeles | London | New Delhi
Singapore | Washington DC

For information:

SAGE Publications, Inc.
2455 Teller Road
Thousand Oaks, California 91320
E-mail: order@sagepub.com

SAGE Publications Ltd.
1 Oliver's Yard
55 City Road
London EC1Y 1SP
United Kingdom

SAGE Publications India Pvt. Ltd.
B 1/I 1 Mohan Cooperative Industrial Area
Mathura Road, New Delhi 110 044
India

SAGE Publications Asia-Pacific Pte. Ltd.
33 Pekin Street #02-01
Far East Square
Singapore 048763

Printed in the United States of America

Library of Congress Cataloging-in-Publication Data

Buckelew, Mary.
Reaching and teaching diverse populations : strategies for moving beyond stereotypes /
Mary Buckelew, Andrea Fishman.
   p. cm.
Includes bibliographical references.
ISBN 978-1-4129-7736-4 (pbk.)

  1. Multicultural education—United States. 2. Educational equalization—United States.
3. Academic achievement—United States. 4. Minorities—Education—United States. I. Fishman,
Andrea. II. Title.

LC1099.B82 2011
370.1170973—dc22   2010031670

This book is printed on acid-free paper.

10 11 12 13 14 10 9 8 7 6 5 4 3 2 1

Acquisitions Editor:	Diane McDaniel
Editorial Assistant:	Ashley Conlon
Production Editor:	Eric Garner
Copy Editor:	Teresa Herlinger
Typesetter:	C&M Digitals (P) Ltd.
Proofreader:	Susan Schon
Cover Designer:	Janet Kiesel
Marketing Manager:	Erica DeLuca

Table of Contents

Preface

Reaching and Teaching Diverse Populations is first and foremost a book for and about students and teachers as individuals. No matter how our classes are identified (upper division, introductory, honors, remedial) and no matter how our students are perceived or labeled (advanced, below basic, ELL, teenage moms), everyone in the classroom is so much more than their category implies. Therefore, the strategies in this book help our students make personal connections to their own and their classmates' multiple identities, enabling them to see the multidimensional nature of individuals, groups, and—especially—the classroom ecosystem as a whole.

Second, this book is designed to complement existing core textbooks that introduce multicultural categories and issues from a global perspective by making those concerns local, i.e., applying them to students' particular cultures and contexts. Rooted in the philosophies of theorists and educators who believe students learn through meaningful experiences, these strategies are interactive, involving dialogue, collaboration, and individual and shared reflection.

Finally, we realize that it takes more than a collection of strategies to reach and teach diverse populations. It takes an inquiry stance, a mind-set that sees the classroom not as a place to impose learning on groups of students but to facilitate learning by each student, recognizing the dynamic, interdependent nature of classroom communities.

The strategies in this book come from our work in K–12, undergraduate, graduate, and professional development settings. They have allowed us to know our students, learn from them, and teach them more effectively as a result. We hope they will do the same for you.

AUDIENCE

This book is designed for four audiences.

1. It is a supplementary text for undergraduate and graduate courses in multicultural education as described above.

2. It is a handbook for both student teachers and veteran teachers interested in moving beyond stereotyped thinking.

3. It is a text for professional development in schools or content-area departments that want to reflect on their own perceptions of multicultural topics and issues.

4. It is a set of strategies for building and sustaining community in any ongoing group or workplace.

ORGANIZATION OF THE TEXT

The strategies in this book are scaffolded to begin where students are—focused on themselves—then move them into interactions with others, first in their classes and then in the field.

Section I begins with **individual identity,** developing self-awareness for all students. They discover the multifaceted—even multicultural—nature of their own identities. They reflect on who they are, what they value, where those identities and values come from, and how the world looks as a result. They articulate what makes them unique individuals, beyond any stereotypes associated with the groups to which they belong.

With awareness of students' individual identities as an explicit foundation, **Section II** addresses **intercultural interaction,** exploring the categories, stereotypes, and lessons proffered by the many cultures in which they live every day. Students move beyond group-think stereotyping by considering the members of any group not just in terms of a single descriptor, but as individuals with multiple identities, just like themselves. In this section, they explicitly address stereotypes and reflect on where such labels come from in order to move beyond them personally and professionally.

Once students understand more about multiculturalism from both individual and interactive perspectives, **Section III** shifts to the process of **classroom inquiry.** Here students learn to view all classrooms as ecosystems, microcosms of multicultural individuals and interactions, no matter how apparently homogenous or overwhelmingly heterogeneous they may appear. This section introduces students to inquiry strategies and processes essential for building inclusive, beyond-stereotypes classroom communities where pedagogy and curriculum are based not just on the teacher's home culture but on the students' communities as well. That makes this section an important connector of preservice students to their soon-to-be professional selves.

Finally, **Section IV** moves to the **implications for practice** of everything students have experienced so far. In this section, students review a set of current best practice strategies probably learned in their methods courses and perhaps experienced as students themselves. They learn four ways to analyze the cultural responsiveness of these strategies, and decide how they might use them to create and sustain their own beyond-stereotypes classrooms as student teachers and in their first professional assignments.

FEATURES OF THE TEXT

STRATEGIES

Most strategies in the book have five parts:

Rationale: a clear explanation of *why* students should use the strategy, what it means, and what it will accomplish;

Step-by-Step Instructions: how to use the strategy, including clear examples, peer interactions, and any materials needed. Where materials are not embedded in the actual activity, a note to the instructor explains where and how to find them.

Looking Back/Looking Ahead: a space in which students consider the experience of the strategy and ways they might use it in their own classrooms;

Content-Area Extensions: ways the strategy can be used or adapted in humanities, science, or related arts classes;

Additional Application: how the strategy can be used for professional development with new or veteran teachers.

FLEXIBLE STRUCTURE

The flexible structure allows you to choose exactly what you need for each course and section you teach. Because we all work in particular campus cultures and contexts and because this book is designed to supplement core texts, the strategies provided here can be done sequentially or individually. Each strategy can (1) stand alone, (2) be paired with strategies from other sections, or (3) be part of a sequence across sections to meet the needs of each semester's classroom community. In addition, many of these strategies can be done in class, for homework, or both, depending on the needs of the instructor and the students (see below for Quick Index Chart).

PROFESSIONAL PORTFOLIO

The professional portfolio component helps students develop as reflective practitioners. Students who use this text will come away from the experience with a professional portfolio they can use immediately in their student teaching and in their first classroom placements. For most completed strategies, students will have both (1) models of the work they produce and (2) their "Looking Back/Looking Ahead" reflections.

VISUAL AIDS

Visual aids serve to illuminate the concepts in each section.

ADDITIONAL RESOURCES

The book also includes the following resources:

- Some strategies include a *Suggestion Box,* offering suggestions for further reading or ways the student or instructor might vary the materials used or the way the strategy might be done.

- A *Quick Index Chart* at the end of this Preface shows which strategies in Sections I and II may be most effectively paired with the most-often identified categories of multicultural education.

- *Readings and sample student work* appear with strategies they support.

- *Other Resources:* Other materials such as student samples can be found on the companion website: **http://www.sagepub.com/buckelew.**

NOTE TO STUDENTS

This text allows you to apply generalized knowledge to your own particular cultures and contexts, both in on-campus studies and fieldwork or professional settings. It will help you experience and then see the implications of theory-in-action, developing the habits-of-mind necessary for reflective practice that moves beyond stereotypes to reach and teach your own diverse populations.

Topic	Section I: Identity & Self-Awareness	Section II: Multicultural Awareness & Intercultural Interaction
Race and Ethnicity	Strategies: 1,2,3, 8,9,10	Strategies: 13,14,15,16,18,19
Class and Socioeconomic Status	Strategies: 2, 6,7, 8,10	Strategies: 13,14,15,16,17,18
Gender and Sexuality Orientation	Strategies: 1,2,3,5, 8,10	Strategies: 13,14,15,16,17,18,19
Exceptionality	Strategies: 2,4,5, 8,9,10	Strategies: 13,14,15
Language	Strategies: 3,4, 7, 8,9,10	Strategies: 15,16,17,19,20
Religion	Strategies: 1,2,6 8, 10	Strategies: 13,14,15,16,17
Geography	Strategies: 2,3,7,8,10	Strategies: 13,14,16,17
Age	Strategies: 3,4,5,7, 8,9,10	Strategies: 13,14,15,16,20
Professional Identity	Strategies: 5,9,11	Strategies: 12,20,21,22
Stereotypes	Strategies: 1,2,5,9,	Strategies: 13,14,16
Community Building	Strategies: 1,2,3,4,5,6,9,11	Strategies: 12,13,15,20

Acknowledgments

We have been inspired and taught by the countless Pennsylvania Writing and Literature Project teachers, teachers in the field, students, and other colleagues we have had the privilege of working with over the years. For their support and belief in the importance of what we do as educators, we offer our heartfelt thanks. We are also grateful for the constant support of our office staff, Ann Mascherino, Toni Kershaw, and Sally Malarney, who keep the wheels of the Writing and Literature Project spinning.

Special thanks are in order for Lyn Fields, Beth Bauer, and their teachers at Wissahickon Middle School and Shady Grove Elementary School for sharing their schools and their vision of reaching and teaching all students with us. We especially want to thank our English 390, 392, and 398 students at West Chester University who helped frame and shape our thinking over the years and allowed us to include their work in our book.

Mary gives a thousand thanks to her family—husband, Paul Perry; son, Sargeant Wil Buckelew; daughter, Clare Buckelew; and mom and dad, Joseph and Jill Bellucci, for their patience, love, and laughter, and to Fred Buckelew who continues to inspire from beyond. She also wishes to thank her GoggleWorks writing group whose encouragement, feedback, and friendship kept her going throughout this process! Many thanks go to Mary's former students from Barrack 33 at West Mesa High School in Albuquerque, New Mexico, who expanded and illuminated her view of the universe and who continue to inspire and inform all that she does. Finally, to Andrea for her partnership, passion, and wisdom—Mary is eternally grateful.

Andrea especially thanks her husband, Bart Pasternak, and son, Matthew Fishman, for their unflagging support and love, regardless of circumstances. She thanks her Pasternak and Caplan children for seeing beyond the stepmother stereotype. She is grateful to the many middle and high school students who learned with and taught her for so many years, and to the Fishers—the remarkable Amish family who first showed her the power of culture and context. And she thanks Mary for being the best professional partner anyone could ever have.

Thank you to our editors, Diane McDaniel and Ashley Conlon, for their encouragement and support. And a special thanks to Steve Wainwright who, at the outset of this project, expressed his genuine interest in the classroom as ecosystem concept.

We would also like to thank the following reviewers for their thoughtful and valuable feedback.

J. Q. Adams,
Western Illinois University

David Bishop,
Northern Kentucky University

Michaelle Kitchen,
Midwestern State University

Anna Kochan,
University of Central Florida

Anne M. Mungai,
Adelphi University

Introduction

The Theoretical Lens for Reaching and Teaching Diverse Populations: The Classroom as Ecosystem

The conceptual framework of the educational ecosystem is the theoretical heart of this text. As you experience the various activities in each section, you may want to revisit this theoretical framework to ponder the dynamics of the individual within the classroom ecosystem and the complexities and implications for reaching and teaching diverse populations. In section III, you will focus on the classroom as ecosystem, but it is valuable to experience the activities with the conceptual framework of the ecosystem in mind.

We have found that students who approach the classroom as an ecosystem to be studied are more apt to see themselves as agents of change, creators of curriculum and pedagogy, and facilitators of an environment that is synergistic and dynamic rather than one that is static and uniform.

WHAT DO WE MEAN BY THE CLASSROOM ECOSYSTEM?

The term *ecosystem* is adapted from biology, where it has long been used to describe the populations of any defined area and their interactions with each other and their shared environment. In recent years, the term has also been used in anthropology, sociology, psychology, economics, political science, and business, frequently differentiated in many of these fields as a "social ecosystem" rather than a biological or ecological one. Current social scientists also add a key word to the definition of ecosystem—*information*—identifying what is exchanged between and among the interdependent organisms. All the contexts of our lives may be thought of as some type of ecosystem, i.e., frames of reference in which we interact with others and with our environment. From the point of view of education, a classroom, a school, and a school district are all educational ecosystems.

Biological Ecosystem	*Classroom Ecosystem*
Abiotic elements—nonliving	Materials, books, curriculum
Biotic elements—living	Humans: teacher, students, aides
Autotrophic elements—independent	Independent learning
Heterotrophic elements—interdependent	Learning interdependent: teacher, students, materials, synergistic, dynamic
Equilibrium—healthy balance	Balanced, safe, comfortable climate/environment
Disequilibrium	Disruptions, chaos
Positive disequilibrium	Debates, discussion

BIOLOGICAL ECOSYSTEM OVERVIEW

Because many students find the visual aspects of the biological ecosystem valuable, we offer a brief overview of some of the biological features, which also metaphorically illuminate the classroom ecosystem.

The following features from the biological model are salient for the classroom ecosystem: abiotic/biotic elements, heterotrophic/autotrophic elements, equilibrium/disequilibrium, positive disequilibrium. An ecosystem is, essentially, the (living, biotic) community inclusive of its (abiotic, but not static) environment and the interdependency inherent in the occurring transactions between and among both the living organisms and nonliving environmental factors.

A classroom, then, can be seen as an ecosystem, a system with an "explicit extent," i.e., a frame within which the biotic components—the students, teacher, aides—and the abiotic components are interdependent. Via the transaction between and among all components, biotic and abiotic learning occurs or information is exchanged. During the exchange, the abiotic (knowledge) and biotic (students and teachers) elements are changed. Further, in ecological terms, one might visualize the autotrophic organism (green plant), which is capable of synthesizing its own nutrients using inorganic light or chemical energy, and the heterotrophic organism (most animals), which is dependent on complex, external organic substances for nutrition. Just as plants autonomously combine inorganic compounds with energy from sunlight, water, and earth to grow and change, students and teachers are capable of synthesizing (analyzing, comprehending) information on their own—whether taking notes, taking tests, or writing essays.

However, the autonomous and interdependent nature of humans and human ecosystems highlights the complexity of the human organism in the educational setting. Just as animals rely on outside substances to grow and change, in the learning environment, teachers and students also rely on outside energy, i.e., social and intellectual exchange and transaction. The classroom, then, can be seen both as an autotrophic zone and heterotrophic zone in that students and teachers are both capable of synthesizing (analyzing, comprehending) information on their own, but in order to learn, they also rely on the social, intellectual, and emotional exchange that occurs in the classroom. See the introduction to Section III for a visual representation.

EDUCATIONAL THEORETICAL CONNECTIONS

Paulo Freire's (1993) problem posing (liberatory) theory of education best represents this dynamic aspect of the information and concept exchange that occurs in the classroom:

> Through dialogue, the teacher-of-the-students and the students-of-the-teacher cease to exist and a new term emerges: teacher-student with students-teachers. The teacher is no longer merely the one-who-teaches, but one who is himself taught in dialogue with the students, who in turn while being taught also teach. They become jointly responsible for a process in which they all grow. (p. 265)

Freire's acknowledgment that "they become jointly responsible for a process in which they all grow" further illustrates the multidimensional aspect of the classroom. His theory clearly supports the classroom as a complex human ecosystem in which the biotic and abiotic transact (ideally) for the benefit of all. Perhaps most important, Freire's perspective encourages the teacher to learn from his or her students, which is exactly what is demanded in the diverse classroom in order to facilitate and sustain the classroom ecosystem.

Learning from and about our students is essential in creating and sustaining equilibrium in the diverse classroom ecosystem. This requires that the teacher do more than acknowledge that there are myriad cultures, attitudes, values, and beliefs on holidays or during Women's History Month. Throughout the year, the teacher must weave in opportunities via pedagogy to create a sustainable ecosystem, one in which equilibrium is a constant. Disequilibrium will occur if we don't come to understand those whose backgrounds differ from our own. Once we come to know each other, we are better able to create an atmosphere in which equilibrium in interactions reigns, but one in which the exchange of ideas among students of diverse backgrounds results in that positive disequilibrium; i.e., excitement and learning result when the exchange of ideas and thoughts are shared in a diverse community. Thus, the ecosystem model may also be used to inform classroom management as we strive to create a classroom environment in which the guidelines for interaction are clear to each individual student so that all students may experience optimal learning.

ELEMENTS OF THE EDUCATIONAL ECOSYSTEM

Organization in the classroom ecosystem is revealed in the nature and kinds of relationships between individuals (e.g., student and teacher, student and student) and between individuals and aspects of the environment (e.g., student and text, teacher and curriculum). In what directions do interactions move in these relationships? Who initiates? Who responds? The flowchart of a thriving, sustainable ecosystem will have arrows moving in a variety of directions instead of all top-down or bottom-up (see the figures that open Sections II and III).

Features of the classroom ecosystem include goals and objectives, rules and procedures, practices and processes, participant roles and functions, leadership roles and functions, values, attitudes, and beliefs. For example, what counts as good reading or good writing? Good teaching or good behavior? Who decides what matters in a given lesson or text? Who decides what something means, what is valued in a classroom, or what attitudes are fostered? What motivates participants?

Principles of operation in a successful classroom ecosystem are similar to those of culturally responsive pedagogy: They make room for and make use of what every student brings to the classroom—their home cultures, background knowledge, and previous experiences. That means that they are

- more collaborative than competitive;

- more organic and multidimensional than mechanical and linear, i.e., derived from rather than imposed on the students (and the teacher);

- more responsive (open and interested) than reactive (closed and theoretically neutral);

- more inclusive than exclusive;

- more win–win than win–lose in the definition of success.

Unlike their scientific counterparts, elements or participants in educational ecosystems cooperate with each other to create, maintain, and support lives and growth. Elements of biological ecosystems are not sentient in the ways people are, i.e., they do not think about, realize, or plan for their connections to or relationships with each other. Each gets what it needs from the others without intention; each provides what the other needs without motive. Participants in the classroom ecosystem are different in this regard, and it is the teacher's responsibility to structure experiences within which supportive, fulfilling, and ultimately motivating interactions can take place for everyone.

If school is a place from which students feel disconnected for whatever reason, they are less likely to want to cooperate there. They need to identify with others, to want to affiliate and cooperate with them rather than separating themselves from the group. Therefore, teachers must ask themselves the following questions:

- What do students need to thrive in this classroom ecosystem?

- What kinds of interactions can I facilitate to meet those needs?

- What do I need to know about my students—and about myself—to create and model effective relationships and a thriving classroom ecosystem?

The strategies in this book are designed to help students and teachers learn what they need to know about themselves and each other to do just that.

SECTION I

Individual Identity and Self-Awareness

Like each organism in the ecosystem, each student is a complex individual with the potential to both contribute to and benefit from interactions with others. Each is shaped by the many social and cultural influences in his or her life to become a distinct human being rather than a stereotype (see Figure I.1). For these reasons, all the strategies in this section are designed to reveal and explore the complex identities of individuals in the diverse classroom, necessary first steps toward building a successful, sustainable ecosystem classroom.

Figure I.1   Influences on Individual Identity Creation

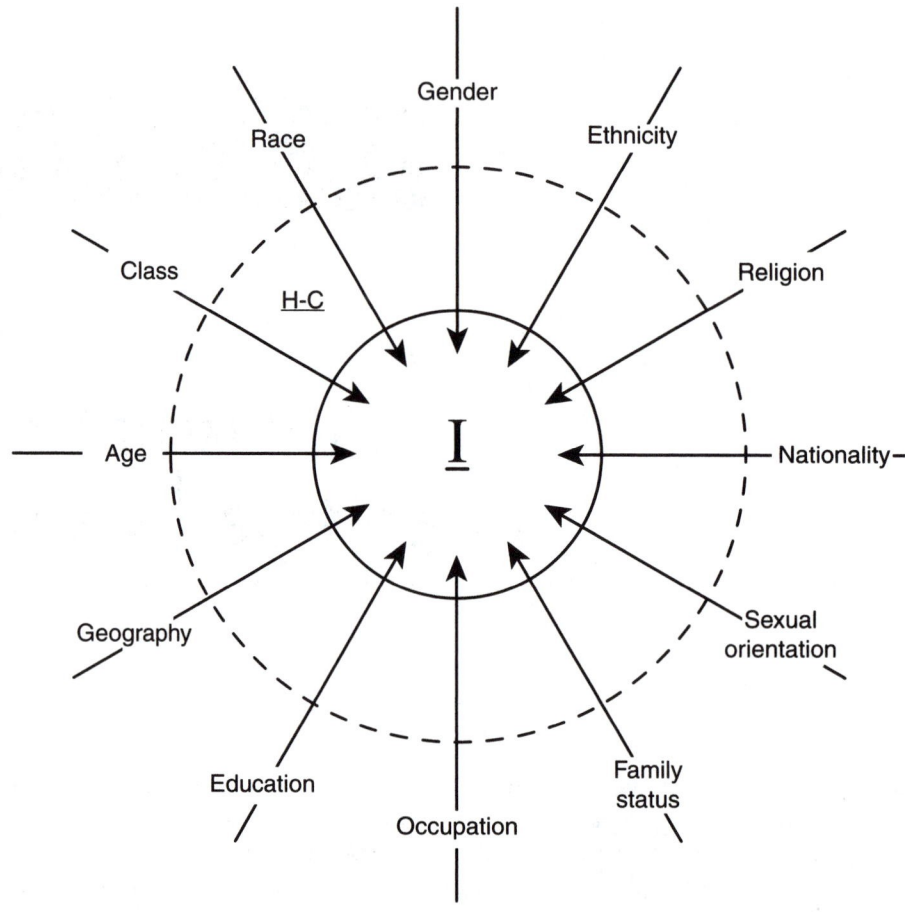

I = the individual teacher or student, bounded by a dotted line/semipermeable membrane through which these influences pass

H-C = the home and communities in which the individual lives outside school; where the I comes from literally

Arrows = features of home and communities from which the individual's values, attitudes, and beliefs come; where the I comes from figuratively

Strategy 1

My Life as a _____

Every student—and teacher—has a life outside the classroom door. They are sons and daughters, brothers and sisters, friends and teammates, and so many other personas who, though not always evident, are always present when they are. In the college or university classroom, students are not often asked to think about who they are or who they are being, which allows them to believe their other-than-student identities are at least private, if not irrelevant. Becoming a teacher, however, requires that you consider the impact all aspects of your personal identities have on your developing professional self.

Consider the two of us. It is impossible for Andrea to deny, for example, that her life as the mother of a son affects her thinking and her teaching. Or to deny that being born and raised in New York City, being a baby boomer, an amateur chef, a newspaper junkie, an iPod novice, an online shopper, a stepmother, and an only child do the same. Likewise, it is impossible for Mary to deny that being the oldest of 10 children; being born and raised in a rural setting; being the mother of two children, a grandmother, an avid reader and traveler, and a dog lover; and leaving home in the East for 25 years in New Mexico inform her teaching and thinking.

This strategy begins making such personal disclosure gently, allowing you to articulate your own multiple identities and to bring more of yourself into the classroom. It acknowledges the many dimensions of your life not included in your identities as "student" and "classmate," and goes beyond the stereotypes associated with more usual identity markers—for example, white boy, black girl, Jew, lesbian—introducing the idea of multicultural identity in an inductive, easily accessed way.

When we do this strategy with students or with teachers, they often react the same way: "I didn't know you _____!" they exclaim to classmates or colleagues, even when they have known each other for years.

STEP-BY-STEP INSTRUCTIONS

1. Write "My life as a _____" at the top of a notebook page. Then list as many ways as you can to fill in the blank.

2. Participate in a class read-around, sharing one item from your list. As you listen to your classmates, add items you forgot until someone else said them. (Don't be surprised if the "Me, too" light goes on frequently as others share. That is exactly what this strategy intends to elicit.)

3. After each student has shared once, repeat the cycle as many times as possible before you or one of your classmates says, "I'm out," meaning he or she has nothing that has not already been said.

4. Pair-share: What did you notice as we did this? What did your partner notice? Jot down a shared list of what was surprising, reassuring, upsetting, puzzling, or any other reaction you experienced.

5. Whole-class discussion: You and your partner share one item from your list. Listen as the other pairs do the same. In what ways is your class diverse? In what ways is it homogeneous?

   What impact have your various identities had on your work as a student? What impact might they have on your work as a teacher?

6. Put your list in your professional portfolio.

LOOKING BACK/LOOKING AHEAD

What was it like to do this strategy? How might you use "My Life as a _____" in your own classroom?

_____

_____

_____

_____

_____

CONTENT-AREA EXTENSIONS

English/Language Arts: This list can be the first page in a writer's notebook, the source of possible topics for any mode of writing.

Reading/Literature: These lists can suggest ways into multicultural literature beyond the usual race, gender, or ethnicity paths.

Social Studies: These identities provide ways to begin talking about how communities are formed and how they interact.

English Language Learners (ELLs): ELLs, those with learning disabilities (LD), and otherwise "identified" students become more than their labels and the expected identities attached.

ADDITIONAL APPLICATION

This strategy helps new teachers meet their colleagues, whether in an induction program or a mixed staff setting. It helps veteran teachers get to know each other in new ways. For both groups, it builds community, making room for more aspects of each person in the building or department. In addition, it helps all teachers consider aspects of their identity that may help—or work against—building relationships with students as well as colleagues.

Strategy 2

I Come From _____*

RATIONALE

While preservice teachers like you are able to self-identify in terms of your roles (as the "My Life as a _____" strategy demonstrates), many students say they have no identifiable culture. This strategy expands the notion of diversity by acknowledging that everyone comes from somewhere specific, particular, different, and special. From the ecosystem perspective, this strategy reveals the interaction of individual and social environments, acknowledging that no one is a self-creation, that everyone is a part of an ecosystem that creates and is created in return.

NOTE TO INSTRUCTOR

When we begin this strategy, we brainstorm with the class before asking students to brainstorm alone. We do this to ensure that students realize that the experiences, people, places, and things we want them to think about are what's special and meaningful to the individual and may range from salad dressing to salvation.

STEP-BY-STEP INSTRUCTIONS

1. Divide a notebook page into four columns or quarters. Label them People, Places, Experiences, and Things.

2. Brainstorm people, places, experiences, and things from your own life that are meaningful to you. They can be big or small, commonplace or unusual. List them in the appropriate categories.

---

*From George Ella Lyons.

For example, under "People," Andrea might include her tenth-grade English teacher as well as her immigrant grandfather. Under "Places," she might list her grandmother's kitchen as well as the summer camp she attended for many years. "Experiences" might include riding her bike through the neighborhood, riding the subway alone for the first time, and reading Nancy Drew mysteries. "Things" could be her grandmother's afghan and her son's first-grade school picture, in addition to other possibilities.

3. Read the sample "I Come From" poems at the end of this strategy.

4. Using your brainstormed ideas as a place to begin, write the first draft of an "I Come From" poem, using the format modeled by the examples.

5. Share your poem with classmates by reading it aloud in a small group or any other way your instructor directs.

6. Whole-class discussion: What do you notice about where your class comes from? What similarities and differences enrich your classroom community?

7. Place your poem in your professional portfolio.

LOOKING BACK/LOOKING AHEAD

What was it like to do this strategy? How might you use "I Come From _____" in your own classroom?

_____

_____

_____

_____

_____

CONTENT-AREA EXTENSIONS

Language Arts: This strategy can be a poetry-writing experience. It can also be a literary analysis strategy when written from the point of view of a character in a piece of literature being studied.

Social Studies: This strategy helps students understand what life is like for people in particular communities or cultures.

Science: "I Come From" poems can be written about animals, plants, even geographic and geologic formations being studied.

Foreign Language: "I Come From" poems can help students explore what it would be like to live in the land of the language being learned.

ADDITIONAL APPLICATION

For new teacher induction programs, this strategy builds a sense of who we in this district are and what we bring to the new shared endeavor. It does the same for veteran teachers, while also helping to explain shared but unexamined history together.

SAMPLE EXCERPTS FROM "I COME FROM" POEMS

I Come From

I come from the rolling hills
Beautifully tinted green
I come from the smell of wet wool
As the sheep pass you on the roads
I come from ruddy faces
Loud laughter pouring from the pubs
And the clunk of your shoes on cobbled streets
I come from a broken nation. . . .
I come from Ireland

I Come From

I come from a baseball team wanting to win
I come from a family not ashamed of their skin

I come from a red-brick ranch house
I come from a family strong at the mouth

I come from a house where my best friend is my brother
I come from a room where I was one with "my cover."
I come from a house full of my hopes and my fears.

Strategy 3

My Name*

Andrea's maiden name was Vigderman. This had two consistent results: She sat in the last row, closer to or further from the back depending on how many Wilsons, Youngs, and Zeiglers there were, and she guessed how much her teachers cared about her by whether they learned to pronounce her name correctly. Even her first name told her that: Those who accented the second syllable were more interested in what they thought than in who she was. Then there was the French teacher who decided she looked "more like a Denise" and called her that for all of ninth grade, much to her consternation.

Individuals are not just names on a roster, nor is classroom learning a solitary pursuit. Each student in a room contributes to—or distracts from—the shared work of sustaining the ecosystem, so the foundation for sharing should be laid early and explicitly. This strategy helps build community early in the semester, allowing you to get to know your classmates both individually and collectively, laying the foundation for more effective communication, interaction, and support throughout the term.

STEP-BY-STEP INSTRUCTIONS

1. Read "My Name," by Sandra Cisneros, found at the end of this strategy.

2. Write about your own name for 8–10 minutes.

3. Pair-share what you've written by reading it aloud to your partner and listening to what he or she has written.

4. Introduce your partner to the class.

5. Whole-class discussion: What did you learn about each other from doing this? What did you learn about yourself?

6. Place your writing in your professional portfolio.

---

*This is a National Writing Project favorite.

LOOKING BACK/LOOKING AHEAD

What was it like to do this strategy? How might you use "My Name" in your own classroom?

_____

_____

_____

_____

CONTENT-AREA EXTENSIONS

Language Arts: This strategy can be used in the study of nomenclature, as connected to semantics or literature.

Social Studies and Foreign Language: This strategy can help students understand the connection between people's names and the cultures they live in.

Science: This strategy can help students understand how different plants, animals, and species got their names.

English Language Learners: These students' more unusual names become explicable and valued, whether in their own or in an inclusion classroom.

ADDITIONAL APPLICATION

This strategy serves the same community-building purpose with any group that will be working together over time. New teachers need to feel seen and known as they begin work in a district. It is also surprising how often veteran teachers, even in the same building, do not know more about their colleagues than what grade or subject they teach. Getting to know each other by name in a meaningful way enhances the shared nature of community and goals, making it easier to work and problem solve together.

MY NAME

By Sandra Cisneros

In English my name means hope. In Spanish it means too many letters. It means sadness, it means waiting. It is like the number nine. A muddy color. It is the Mexican records my father plays on Sunday mornings when he is shaving, songs like sobbing.

It was my great-grandmother's name and now it is mine. She was a horse woman too, born like me in the Chinese year of the horse—which is supposed to be bad luck if you're born female—but I think this is a Chinese lie because the Chinese, like the Mexicans, don't like their women strong.

My great-grandmother. I would've liked to have known her, a wild horse of a woman, so wild she wouldn't marry until my great-grandfather threw a sack over her head and carried her off. Just like that, as if she were a fancy chandelier. That's the way he did it.

And the story goes she never forgave him. She looked out the window all her life, the way so many women sit their sadness on an elbow. I wonder if she made the best with what she got or was she sorry because she couldn't be all the things she wanted to be. Esperanza. I have inherited her name, but I don't want to inherit her place by the window.

At school they say my name funny as if the syllables were made out of tin and hurt the roof of your mouth. But in Spanish my name is made out of a softer something, like silver, not quite as thick as sister's name Magdalena which is uglier than mine. Magdalena who at least can come home and become Nenny. But I am always Esperanza.

I would like to baptize myself under a new name, a name more like the real me, the one nobody sees. Experanza as Lisandra or Maritza or Zeze the X. Yes. Something like Zeze the X will do.

Metaphorical Me

The Grab Bag

Strategy 4

RATIONALE

Just as people often make snap judgments about others based on appearance and superficial behaviors, we often do the same to ourselves. The fraternity sweatshirt or team hat that you wear, and the people you sit with in the cafeteria or party with on Friday night, may provide a mirror image of—but not a window into—who you are.

This strategy uses metaphor as a heuristic to expand your self-awareness beyond the obvious. You will reflect upon your personal attributes in terms of an inanimate object, which will help you to move beyond surface features to deeper characteristics of which you may not be as aware. While our students often have fun with this strategy, they also begin to appreciate the diversity of personal attributes among their classmates who might appear to dress, look, and speak the same language.

In addition to asking you to consider your own personal attributes, this strategy demonstrates the importance of looking beyond the surface features of your future students in order to create a classroom ecosystem that is responsive to all individuals. You will explore multidimensional aspects of yourself, so that you will be better prepared to look beyond the physical and outer appearances of your future students to see the person within each and every one of them.

NOTE TO INSTRUCTOR

This strategy requires some variation of the household objects listed below. You may require students to bring an object to class as noted in the Step-by-Step Instructions or bring in enough objects for the entire class yourself. You will need to bring a tote bag, box, or some receptacle in which to place the objects—preferably, a receptacle in which the objects are not visible.

MATERIALS

Bring an object from home or use an object from your backpack. The objects may be as common and disparate as a light bulb, key, pet leash, conch shell, duct tape, rock, mug, spool of thread, stapler, or a pad of Post-it notes.

STEP-BY-STEP INSTRUCTIONS

1. Place your object in the box, tote bag, or other receptacle provided by your instructor.

2. When the receptacle is passed to you, without looking inside, select an object other than your own.

3. Study your object. Note both the surface attributes and the unseen attributes.

4. List as many attributes of the item as you can in your notebook or journal.

   For example, Mary's student selected a roll of gray duct tape and listed the following attributes: gray, soft, sticky, round, strong, reliable, utilitarian, practical, useful, holds things together, covers cracks, and so on.

5. List some similarities between your object's attributes and your own personality/attributes that might not be obvious to someone who doesn't know you. For example, this student wrote "gray," and next to it she wrote, "Sometimes I have gray days (moody); practical = I am a practical person. I don't rush into things. Holds things together = my family tells me I hold them together." You may also list ways in which you are *not* like your object, e.g., not practical, not gray like the duct tape.

6. Develop an analogy using five or more sentences in your notebook.

   For example, here's an excerpt from the above student: "Some people may not realize just how much I am like this duct tape. On certain days I feel a bit gray just like the color of this duct tape. I also might seem a bit moody and cranky but like the outside of the duct tape I'm also soft and sensitive . . . I hold things together, and I'm also very strong like this duct tape. My family tells me that I hold them together through thick and thin times. I'm also reliable, steady, and strong. However, I'm not round but straight and narrow when it comes to my physical appearance."

7. Pair-share with classmate or in small groups, by reading—not telling—what you wrote.

8. Whole-class discussion: What surprised you about your pair-share partner or other classmates? What similarities and differences enrich your classroom ecosystem?

LOOKING BACK/LOOKING AHEAD

In a few sentences, reflect upon your experience with this strategy. What did you notice? What surprised you? Now explain how you might use this strategy in your future classroom.

_____

_____

_____

_____

_____

CONTENT-AREA EXTENSIONS

Science/Math: In a science or mathematics unit on crystals and their properties/attributes, display a variety of crystals that the students have studied. Possibilities include the following: barite, pyrite, silver, gold, diamond, garnet, galena, topaz, calcite, gypsum, turquoise, quartz, and zircon.

Science: When studying the animal or plant kingdom, ask students to choose one or two animals or plants on which to become experts. Then ask them to draw comparisons between the attributes of one of the animals or plants and themselves.

Math: Have students choose the vocabulary or objects from a math lesson, e.g., triangle, rectangle, octagon in Step 1 above; skip Step 2.

History: Have students choose artifacts from the era the class is studying in Step 1; skip Step 2.

English Language Learners: The above lesson is an excellent way to reinforce vocabulary and deepen understanding of figurative language, which often poses problems for non-native speakers.

ADDITIONAL APPLICATION

New and veteran teachers can use this strategy in a variety of ways. It can serve as an ice breaker and community builder. They can consider how they might use it in their own classrooms or make connections to other strategies they use or have observed.

Professional Identity Collage

Strategy 5

Whether on Facebook, MySpace, or some other 21st-century web venue, many of you may share facets of your identities with friends and strangers alike. From blog postings to pictures to podcasts, personal identity is made public via the web. This collage strategy shifts the focus from the personal self with which many students are so comfortable to the professional self, which you may have yet to consider. This strategy recognizes the complexity of integrating those two identities in constructive ways, providing an opportunity to visualize the emergence of a professional self and a basis for beginning discussion of the following questions: Who do I want to be as a teacher? What values, attitudes, and beliefs do I want to model? Which theories do I plan to take with me to the classroom ecosystem? What is too personal in the classroom?

When Mary does this strategy, she shares the beginnings of her own professional identity collage in order to focus the strategy. She includes pictures of books because she teaches writing and literature courses and because she's a book lover. She includes words like *respect, diversity,* and *honesty* on her poster because she values these concepts in her own classroom. She includes lines from favorite authors and favorite theorists because those, too, are personal choices directly connected to her professional life. A picture of herself—or another woman—in a suit would suggest how she literally sees herself in the classroom. She might also include artwork because she thinks integrating the curriculum is so important.

Creating professional collages allows you and your classmates to continue to expand and examine your perspectives on your own multidimensional selves while broadening your perceptions of the world and your place in it, so that you—in turn—can do the same for your future students.

From an ecosystem perspective, this strategy reveals how different ecosystems require that we foreground different aspects of ourselves in order to navigate different systems successfully. In the case of your professional life as a teacher, there will be some aspects of your life and yourself that you will move to the foreground and others that you will keep in the background in order to create a culturally responsive classroom. Creating your professional collage further demonstrates the importance of providing your future students with the opportunities to learn about and from each other.

NOTE TO INSTRUCTOR

You may want to check out the sample collages on the companion website: **http://www .sagepub.com/buckelew**.

MATERIALS

Poster board, magazines, glue sticks, markers, 3 × 5 index cards. If technology is available, you may want to create a computer-generated collage rather than a paper poster and save it to a DVD so that you can share it with your classmates. See **http:// www.sagepub.com/buckelew**, noted above, for student samples.

STEP-BY-STEP INSTRUCTIONS

1. Brainstorm a list of anything that you think might in some way inform your professional teaching life. For example, a student might list his love of music and its connection to his teaching life. Other possibilities might include quotations that will inspire your teaching life; the names of educational theorists or content-area gurus; as well as the values, attitudes, and beliefs that you will take to your classroom ecosystem.

2. Find pictures, symbols, words, or quotations that will convey your professional self to your classmates in a colorful and artistic manner.

3. Create your professional collage on poster board or on the computer (DVD).

4. Exchange your collage with a classmate. Interpret your classmate's collage. On the 3 × 5 card, write your interpretation or understanding of your partner's professional self.

5. Share your interpretations and your explanations. Discuss commonalities and differences in how you see your professional selves.

6. Display collages. Place around the room.

7. Whole-class discussion: Discuss anything you noticed.

8. Place collage in your professional portfolio.

LOOKING BACK/LOOKING AHEAD

In a few sentences, reflect upon your experience with this strategy. What did you notice? What surprised you? Now explain how you might use this in your future classroom.

_____

_____

_____

_____

_____

CONTENT-AREA EXTENSIONS

English/Language Arts/History: The professional identity collage can be used with literature, both fiction and nonfiction, to create character/historical figure collages that demonstrate student comprehension of the multidimensional aspect of characterization or the individual.

Science: Students can create organism collages that illustrate the features of a variety of objects of scientific study.

ADDITIONAL APPLICATION

This strategy gives new and veteran teachers the opportunity to learn more about each other while also engaging in self-analysis. The collage strategy also functions as a community builder.

Strategy
6

Zen Cards

RATIONALE

Whether secular or religious, every student—and teacher—brings myriad beliefs and perspectives to the classroom. These perspectives bear examining in light of the classroom ecosystem so that you can begin thinking about how your beliefs will inform your future practice with diverse populations. The Zen card strategy is a first step in making transparent those perspectives that may be productive, counterproductive, or need revision for teaching in a diverse setting.

The Zen card deck contains 50 cards with 50 different words printed on them—words such as Success, Community, Courage, or Clarity. On the flip side of each card, there is an accompanying phrase that illuminates the word. For example, a card may have the word "Community" printed on one side, and on the flip side the accompanying phrase, "Understand that you will be like those with whom you surround yourself. Your environment is stronger than you are." In responding to this particular card, you would think of your own beliefs about community and how that belief might impact your navigation of the universe and finally your future classroom. For instance, one of Mary's students wrote the following response to the Community card:

> I think this statement is partially true because the people we surround ourselves with are usually people who have similar interests like we do. While this is a good thing, it's also important to step outside of our comfort zones to find out what others think. For example in my biology class, the professor places us in different groups so that we aren't always sharing responses to the readings with the same people or our friends, and I was surprised and shocked by the variety of responses in my group to Darwinism; it was amazing and interesting. . . . When I have my own classroom, I'll remember that it's important to create a community of learners as we've discussed in Ed. 103, but I'll also remember that hearing diverse ideas is just as important, so I'll rearrange groups throughout the year.

The Zen card strategy allows you to individually explore your beliefs in relation to the philosophical statement found on your card, furthering the progression from the personal to the professional self. In addition, because we tend to sit in the same groups or with friends, this strategy is also especially effective for community building, i.e., you will learn more about your classmates and the varied perspectives of those you might not otherwise have gotten to know beyond a surface level, further strengthening the classroom ecosystem.

NOTE TO INSTRUCTOR

Prior to class, count out enough cards for each student. The cards come in five colors. In a class of 20 students, for example, select four cards from each of the five colors. Place the appropriate number of Zen cards in a receptacle. Follow the steps below.

MATERIALS

Zen Cards by Daniel Levin, ISBN number 1-5617-0804-6

STEP-BY-STEP INSTRUCTIONS

1. Select a card by reaching into the box/basket without looking.

2. Write down the word and phrase from your Zen card.

3. Write a response to your card. You might begin by writing a general response such as how the phrase or word connects or does not connect to your own life (social, personal, school) and then move from the personal to the professional. For example, how might the phrase or word relate to your future classroom?

4. Gather in groups according to the color of your cards.

5. Small groups: Select a timekeeper who will make sure that everyone has a chance to share. One person begins by reading his or her card to the group, followed by his or her response (2–3 minutes). The others then respond to what is read for no more than 2 minutes. Follow this procedure until everyone has had a chance to read and respond. (Total time: 15 minutes)

6. Whole-class discussion: Discuss connections to your philosophy of teaching and learning, classroom ecosystem, and students.

7. Place response (#3) in your professional portfolio.

LOOKING BACK/LOOKING AHEAD

In a few sentences, reflect upon your experience with this strategy. What did you notice? What surprised you? Now explain how you might use this in your future classroom.

_____

_____

_____

_____

_____

Content-Area Extensions

Science: Science teachers can create color-coded cards based on a unit of study. For example, if you are studying the ecosystem, you might use the words heterotrophic, autotrophic, community, interdependence, and so on.

Humanities: A former student who was teaching a unit on Plato, Socrates, and Aristotle created her own color-coded cards using quotations from each philosopher. Students had to ascribe each quotation to a philosopher and explain why in a brief paragraph. She then reconfigured students by the color of their cards so that there was an Aristotle, Plato, and Socrates in each group. Students shared their cards with the other group members. Once finished, they had a whole-class discussion to ensure that all students had correctly identified the philosopher with the corresponding card.

Additional Application

This strategy serves the same purpose with new and veteran teachers—it builds community and gives teachers the opportunity to think more deeply about their beliefs and the impact of those beliefs on the classroom.

Reading Worlds Into Words*

*Source: Adapted from Sheridan Blau, *The Literature Workshop*. Portsmouth, NH: Heinemann. 2003.

RATIONALE

Studying difference from the perspective of groups or cultures is like studying a neighborhood from a helicopter. The view from 10,000 feet may provide an outline of broad parameters—the number and kinds of houses and cars on a block; the number and perhaps genders of adults and children walking around or in their backyards—but it offers only a superficial, often stereotypical view of the individuals who live there. From 10,000 feet, all New Yorkers, Koreans, senior citizens—members of any group— look very much alike. To understand what it means to actually be one of these people requires the view from the ground.

This strategy asks you to not only take a ground-level view of others, but to also put yourself in someone else's place, to understand the environment and relationships from his or her perspective. The strategy can be done with many different kinds of texts. History, sociology, education, anthropology, and literature—most humanities disciplines—offer descriptions of families or other groups living in particular places at particular times. This strategy has three goals: (1) for you to understand what it is or was like to be some- one other than yourself; (2) for you to explore where your own views of others come from; and (3) for you to realize that your reading of both words and worlds is a prod- uct of your own particular experience and resulting perspective, which may or may not coincide with that of others with whom you share the classroom ecosystem.

Because our experience suggests that the level of detail in imaginative literature provides eas- ier access to the lives of others—and because a short poem can be as effective as a long essay or short story—this model uses "My Papa's Waltz," a poem by Theodore Roethke, originally published in 1942. The strategy can be done with excerpts from autobiographies or memoirs or with children's books as well. See the Suggestion Box below for specific possibilities.

STEP-BY-STEP INSTRUCTIONS

1. Read "My Papa's Waltz," found at the end of this strategy.

2. Identify the three roles—points of view—the poet offers in his account of this incident.

3. Consider how each of these individuals could view the experience they shared. For example, the speaker might say, "I was so excited when my papa came home from work before I went to bed." Or he or she could say, "I was so scared when my papa came home before I went to bed."

4. Choose one of the three points of view and write a first-person account of the incident in which you describe what happened and explain what you felt, thought, and believed about it both during and after the waltz.

5. Meet with other students who chose the same point of view you did, i.e., the speakers, fathers, and mothers each form their own groups. Read your account aloud and listen to your classmates'.

6. After hearing everyone's account, discuss what might explain differences in your perceptions of the same experience. Why, for example, might some students believe the father is abusive while others believe he is loving, if somewhat clumsy? Why might some believe the mother is angry while others believe she's hard-pressed but tolerant? Why might some believe the speaker is frightened while others believe he or she is exhilarated? Why do some believe the speaker is a boy? A girl?

7. As a class, discuss what A-List and B-List categories explain different perceptions of the poem's family and their shared experience. (See Section II, Strategy 2 for these lists.) How do these categorical differences explain conflicts in how people "read the world," in Paulo Freire's (1993) terms, as well as how they read texts? What positive—and negative—impact might such differences make in a classroom?

8. Place your point-of-view writing in your professional portfolio.

LOOKING BACK/LOOKING AHEAD

What was it like to do this strategy? How might you use "Reading Worlds Into Words" in your own classroom?

_____

_____

_____

_____

_____

CONTENT-AREA EXTENSIONS

Humanities: Teachers can choose texts that reflect the period, culture, or group they are studying.

English Language Learners (ELLs): ELL teachers can use this as a way for their students to connect their own lives and cultures to their content areas.

ADDITIONAL APPLICATION

This strategy works similarly with groups of new and veteran teachers.

SUGGESTION BOX

Children's books that work well with this strategy include *Nappy Hair* by Carolivia Herron; *The Honest-to-Goodness Truth* by Patricia McKissack; *Pink and Say* by Patricia Polacco; and *The Other Side* by Jacqueline Woodson.

MY PAPA'S WALTZ

By Theodore Roethke

The whiskey on your breath
Could make a small boy dizzy;
But I hung on like death:
Such waltzing was not easy.

We romped until the pans
Slid from the kitchen shelf;
My mother's countenance
Could not unfrown itself.

The hand that held my wrist
Was battered on one knuckle;
At every step you missed
My right ear scraped a buckle.

You beat time on my head
With a palm caked hard by dirt,
Then waltzed me off to bed
Still clinging to your shirt.

Strategy 8

Stories That Cling*

RATIONALE

While a person's values, attitudes, and beliefs may be shaped initially by explicit teaching both at home and in his or her community, they are tested, affirmed, and reshaped by individual life experiences. In fact, most adults remember some "Aha" moment when they learned something they will never forget. These are not necessarily "big" moments, like high school graduation or the death of a loved one, nor even "middle-size" moments like winning the class spelling bee or spraining an ankle the day before the prom. They may be small moments, like being forgiven—or not forgiven—by your mother for breaking your grandmother's crystal pitcher, or having a teacher who always mispronounced your name.

Remembering these stories helps you begin to think about *why* you value what you value and believe what you believe, and often prompts reflection on whether those values, attitudes, and beliefs are truly yours, truly valid, and truly useful in the present moment and current environment. Sharing these stories helps individuals appreciate how other people come to their understandings of the world, and how both individual and universal the development of values, attitudes, and beliefs can be.

It should be noted that these stories often begin to raise what Paulo Freire has termed a "critical consciousness," as you and your classmates begin to question the social worldviews you each inherited as well as the worldviews of others. The generative themes these stories contain can be pursued at any time in a course. We pursue them more explicitly in Sections II and III.

STEP-BY-STEP INSTRUCTIONS

1. Read the sample "story that clings," found at the end of this strategy.

2. Brainstorm/list stories that cling to you from your home, community, or school life.

---

*The phrase "stories that cling" comes from Ibsen's dramatic poem *Peer Gynt*, in which a mother fills her child's head with "fairy stories" in an attempt to protect him from reality. When the stories have unanticipated consequences, she wonders, "Who would have thought the stories would cling to him so?"

3. Choose one incident from your list and write that story in as much detail as possible. (Be aware that you will share your story in a small group, so do not write anything you would not want others to know.)

4. Read your story aloud to a small group of classmates and listen to theirs.

5. Small-group discussion: What was it like to share your story? To hear others'?

6. Whole-class discussion: How does sharing individual stories as classmates or as instructor and students impact the classroom community? What kinds of guidelines, structures, or other scaffolds might you use when you ask your own students to share stories?

7. Place your story in your professional portfolio.

LOOKING BACK/LOOKING AHEAD

What was it like to do this strategy? How might you use "Stories That Cling" in your own classroom?

_____

_____

_____

_____

_____

CONTENT-AREA EXTENSIONS

Language Arts: Stories that cling are appropriate for teaching narrative writing, memoir, and the personal essay. They also help readers connect their lives to those of characters they encounter in fiction or subjects of nonfiction. For both writing and literature, they provide a lens for thinking about behavior/character development, motivation, and foreshadowing.

Social Studies: Most cultures have their own stories that cling. Everything from Greek myths to scripture, Paul Bunyan to Horatio Alger fits in this category. When studying a particular culture, it is useful to consider how such stories shape and express that culture's values, attitudes, and beliefs.

ADDITIONAL APPLICATION

With preservice teachers, the stories may come from any time or place in their lives as they straddle the student–teacher divide. For new teacher induction, however, it may be more useful to frame these as "tales out of school," coming from their experiences as students or their recent experience as teachers to focus on their potential impact as professionals. For veteran teachers, either approach might be appropriate, depending on the purpose of the staff development or graduate course at hand.

SAMPLE "STORY THAT CLINGS"

Lawrence "Larry" Cavenaugh-McConnell [not his real name] seemed like the ideal student. This slightly older, nontraditional preservice teacher was always attentive, engaged, and responsive. Larry willingly participated in difficult discussions of race, ethnicity, religion, and class by articulating and questioning his own Irish Catholic, working-class values, attitudes, and beliefs. Never shy, always inquisitive, Larry seemed likely to become a model teacher in what some would call post-racial America—until the day I introduced the course segment on gender by considering sexist language that often goes unaddressed, that is.

I divided the class in half, asking one group to list all the synonyms they could think of for "woman," the other group for "man." As I anticipated, the list for "woman" was longer and much less flattering than its male counterpart. The most troubling words were not the sexual ones, my female students agreed. The most troubling words were the assumed terms of endearment. Words like "honey," "sweetie," "cookie," and "babe" offended many of the women in the room because they seemed so demeaning. "I work as a waitress," one female student acknowledged, "and I hate it when men [customers] think those are compliments. They are not!" As other women chimed in with similar experiences and perspectives, I could see Larry's usually open face begin to close. Finally, he couldn't stand it.

"Wait a minute!" he exclaimed. "There's nothing wrong with those words! I call my wife 'sweetie' and 'honey' all the time. Are you saying I'm a sexist? I am not sexist!"

Larry's class participation was never the same after that. By the end of the semester, only a few weeks after this outburst, he had rebuilt his relationships with classmates, but he had clearly never forgiven me for "mousetrapping" him with that strategy. "There had to be a better way you could have introduced sexism," he wrote in his final course evaluation. "You didn't have to make me look bad. And I still don't think those words are sexist."

Larry was right. There was a better way. I just never imagined I would need one, especially where my most open-minded, inquisitive student was concerned. Besides, the strategy I used seemed self-evidently neutral to me. Focused on language, done in the third person (i.e., I didn't ask them what words *they* use; I asked what words *are* used), we would look at mainstream and popular American culture together, and surely we would agree. Now I credit Larry with opening my mind to the reality that I can't know or predict what will make a student defensive; what will shut him—or her—down; or what will become more object lesson than model for reaching and teaching a diverse student population, even when they don't appear all that diverse. In other words, I credit Larry with putting me on the road to this book.

—*Andrea Fishman*

Ways of Seeing

Beyond First Impressions

Strategy 9

For the artist creation begins with vision. To see is itself a creative operation requiring an effort. Everything that we see in our daily life is more or less distorted by acquired habit.

—Henri Matisse

This Matisse quotation raises questions important for you as a future teacher: How do I see the world in which I live in relation to myself? What habits of seeing have I acquired and how do they influence my perception of others? How might these habits impact my field observations? My future classroom? My students?

This strategy continues the progression from personal to professional. It gives you and your classmates the opportunity to look through another metaphorical lens—a painting—to examine your ways of seeing; to continue to move beyond stereotyping; and finally to see your own transaction with the various ecosystems in which you find yourself on a daily basis. Getting beyond stereotypes means seeing beyond the surface features of a person, a painting, or an object. As Matisse notes, to see is itself a "creative operation requiring effort," so in our teaching lives we must be extra vigilant in seeing beyond the surface. From an ecosystem perspective, this strategy provides a lens for you to reflect on the individual—in this case, yourself—and your interaction n one or more ecosystems. It helps build community, allowing you to know your classmates both individually and collectively when you share your responses throughout the strategy.

NOTE TO INSTRUCTOR

This strategy works best with abstract art. You may want to order your own set of art postcards prior to doing this strategy, or ask students to find an abstract painting on the

Internet or in the library to bring to class. We recommend Wassily Kandinsky's work, available as postcards on the Internet. You might try *Wassily Kandinsky: Prestel Postcard Book,* ISBN 3-7913-3128-0; or *Kandinsky Watercolors: Prestel Postcard Book,* ISBN: 3-7913-1356-8.

MATERIALS

1. Receptacle/box/basket.

2. Bring enough art postcards or pictures for the entire class, or have each student bring one.

   (Suggested artists: Wassily Kandinsky, Henri Matisse, Diego Rivera, Gustav Klimt, Frieda Kahlo, Lee Krasner, Georgia O'Keefe.)

STEP-BY-STEP INSTRUCTIONS

1. Divide a notebook page into four columns or quarters.

2. Label the columns as follows: Column 1: Initial Response (4–5 sentences); Column 2: First Read (list); Column 3: My life is like/not like or both (5–10 sentences); Column 4: Reflection (5–10 sentences). Specific directions for each column follow below.

3. Place postcards or pictures in a box, tote bag, or other receptacle in which the objects are not visible.

4. Pass the receptacle and without looking inside, select a postcard/painting other than your own, *or* the instructor will randomly distribute art postcards.

5. Column 1: Initial Response—Study the painting that you selected. Then take a few minutes to record your initial reaction. For example, were you immediately drawn to your painting? If so, why? Would you want to hang this in your apartment? Dorm room?

6. Column 2: First Read—In this column, list just the facts. You do not need to make meaning of the work at this point—you just want to notice its surface features. For instance, one of Mary's students listed the following for his Kandinsky art postcard: pinkish brush strokes, bright yellow circle, black square, red sun shape, royal blue line, navy blue circle, straight lines, jagged lines, zig-zag lines, circles, half circle, and triangles. Once you have listed 10 or more features for your card, move on to the next step.

7. Column 3: My life is like—Write an analogy in paragraph form, using 5–10 sentences. Use one or more of the following stems: "My (social, school, family, professional) life is like this painting because . . ." or "My life is not like this painting because . . ." or "My life is both like and not like this painting

because . . ." For example, here is an excerpt from one of Mary's students: "My painting is filled with bright colors—reds, yellows, pinks. My life at home and school [is] usually cheerful combinations of brightness and excitement and on most days that's how I feel: cheerful, optimistic about life and the future. However, the placement of the shapes has a rather chaotic appearance, and on some days, I'm overwhelmed with my school work and job, and I feel scattered and chaotic like the zigging and zagging of the lines, looking for direction."

8. Pair-share with a classmate. Read your paragraphs to each other. Select phrases that stand out in your partner's piece and tell him or her what they are.

9. Column 4: Reflection—Look back to Column 1. How has your reaction to your painting changed? Why has it changed? What surprised you about the strategy?

10. Whole-class discussion: Share your responses from Column 4. What connections can you make between your initial response, the process, and your future students? How might the different perspectives shared impact your future classrooms? What does this strategy have to do with moving beyond stereotypes?

11. Place your responses in your professional portfolio.

LOOKING BACK/LOOKING AHEAD

In a few sentences, reflect upon your experience with this strategy. What did you notice? What surprised you? How might you use this in your future classroom?

_____

_____

_____

_____

_____

CONTENT-AREA EXTENSIONS

Reading: This strategy can be used to illustrate or reinforce reading and writing strategies across the disciplines. See References and Suggested Readings for articles that extend this strategy.

English/Art/Humanities: The art postcard strategy can serve as a springboard into a variety of research projects on the artist, the genre of art depicted in the painting, the historical or cultural period of art, or the art form.

ADDITIONAL APPLICATION

Both new and veteran teachers can make connections between their postcards and their classrooms, their students, or their schools and professional lives. For example, "My students are like this painting because ...."; "My classroom is like this painting because ....."; "My life as principal of Smith Middle School is like/not like this painting because ....."

Willing to Be Disturbed

Strategy 10

- I don't see color when I look at my students.

- God loves everyone, but you have to accept Jesus to go to heaven.

- Muslims are the enemy of America.

- Don't ask, don't tell. That's the best policy.

- Men are from Mars. Women are from Venus.

- Anyone can be successful if they just try hard enough.

- I know what it's like to be a minority. I volunteered to help paint an all-black high school on Martin Luther King Day one year. I was the only white person there.

These, like most beliefs, seem self-evident to the people who believe them. They seem neutral and objective, because in believers' eyes they are facts and, therefore, true. Expecting people with beliefs like these to see their connection to racism, sexism, anti-Semitism, classism, or ethnocentrism means expecting them to turn their worlds upside down simply because textbooks or instructors tell them to do so.

Because teacher preparation has embraced America's multicultural reality, however, this expectation may seem reasonable from a curricular perspective. Preservice teachers like you—and even veteran teachers—need to learn the terminology of pluralism and understand the issues embedded in "isms" of all kinds. You need to know how these ideologies shape the sociopolitical landscape of American education. Equity, democracy, and anti-racist education are hallmarks of successful 21st-century teachers, classrooms, and schools.

Despite this curricular rationale, these ideas remain both personally fundamental and potentially disturbing, which makes your willingness to be disturbed crucial to your learning. In this strategy, being disturbed becomes both acceptable and desirable. It shows how change—disequilibrium within an individual or a group—while difficult, is also useful, manageable, and an opportunity to solve problems that arise in both personal and professional settings. It allows you to acknowledge your discomfort and to use it as something that connects you to—rather than separates you from—your professional and personal goals.

Step-by-Step Instructions

1. Read Margaret Wheatley's essay "Willing to Be Disturbed," found at the end of this strategy.

2. Use the double-entry journal form at the end of this strategy to scaffold your active reading of the essay to prepare for focused discussion.

3. In small groups, share the journal entry you would most like to think about further.

4. Group members play "the believing game," i.e., if Wheatley is right, what does that mean for us as individuals and as a profession when it comes to dealing with issues of multiculturalism?

5. Whole-class discussion: How should we as individuals and as a class use Wheatley's ideas in this course? In our field observations? In student teaching?

6. Place your responses in your professional portfolio.

Looking Back/Looking Ahead

What was it like to do this strategy? How might you use "Willing to Be Disturbed" in your own classroom?

_____

_____

_____

_____

_____

Content-Area Extensions

Language Arts: Literature often disturbs students, especially when characters and settings are unfamiliar. Playing the believing game can help them connect with the unfamiliar. It also provides a perspective that informs persuasive, argumentative, or informational writing, including research papers.

Social Studies: Units on slavery, civil rights, or the Holocaust can be very disturbing to students. The concepts in this strategy can make that disturbance explicit and legitimate, using students' own reactions as a basis for understanding history's relevance to their lives.

ADDITIONAL APPLICATION

New teacher induction programs can use this as an inquiry thread for all participants as they move through their first years in the profession. A Willing to Be Disturbed Journal (or simply a Disturbances Journal) can be the source of ongoing discussion, writing topics, or think-tank protocol material. (See Section III for protocol step-by-step instructions.)

Veteran teachers in professional development or graduate programs will benefit similarly. For them, however, this may be more difficult as it challenges practices of an established career.

WILLING TO BE DISTURBED

By Margaret J. Wheatley

As we work together to restore hope to the future, we need to include a new and strange ally—our willingness to be disturbed. Our willingness to have our beliefs and ideas challenged by what others think. No one person or perspective can give us the answers we need to the problems of today. Paradoxically, we can only find those answers by admitting we don't know. We have to be willing to let go of our certainty and expect ourselves to be confused for a time.

We weren't trained to admit we don't know. Most of us were taught to sound certain and confident, to state our opinion as if it were true. We haven't been rewarded for being confused. Or for asking more questions rather than giving quick answers. We've also spent many years listening to others mainly to determine whether we agree with them or not. We don't have time or interest to sit and listen to those who think differently than we do.

But the world now is quite perplexing. We no longer live in those sweet, slow days when life felt predictable, when we actually knew what to do next. We live in a complex world, we often don't know what's going on, and we won't be able to understand its complexity unless we spend more time in not knowing.

It is very difficult to give up our certainties—our positions, our beliefs, our explanations. These help define us; they lie at the heart of our personal identity. Yet I believe we will succeed in changing this world only if we can think and work together in new ways. Curiosity is what we need. We don't have to let go of what we believe, but we do need to be curious about what someone else believes.

We do need to acknowledge that their way of interpreting the world might be essential to our survival.

We live in a dense and tangled global system. Because we live in different parts of this complexity, and because no two people are physically identical, we each experience life differently. It's impossible for any two people to ever see things exactly the same. You can test this out for yourself. Take any event that you've shared with others (a speech, a movie, a current event, a major problem) and ask your colleagues and friends to describe their interpretations of that event. I think you'll be amazed at how many different explanations you'll hear. Once you get a sense of diversity, try asking even more colleagues. You'll end up with a rich tapestry of interpretations that are much more interesting than any single one.

To be curious about how someone else interprets things, we have to be willing to admit that we're not capable of figuring things out alone. If our solutions don't work as well as we want them to, if our explanations of why something happened don't feel sufficient, it's time to begin asking others what they see and think. When so many interpretations are available, I can't understand why we would be satisfied with superficial conversations where we pretend to agree with one another.

There are many ways to sit and listen for the differences. Lately, I've been listening for what surprises me. What did I just hear that startled me? This isn't easy—I'm accustomed to sitting there nodding my head to those saying things I agree with. But when I notice what surprises me, I'm able to see my own views more clearly, including my beliefs and assumptions.

Noticing what surprises and disturbs me has been a very useful way to see invisible beliefs. If what you say surprises me, I must have been assuming something else was true. If what you say disturbs me, I must believe something contrary to you. My shock at your position exposes my own position. When I hear myself saying, "How could anyone believe something like that?" a light comes on for me to see my own beliefs. These moments are great gifts. If I can see my beliefs and assumptions, I can decide whether I still value them.

I hope you'll begin a conversation listening for what's new. Listen as best you can for what's different, for what surprises you. See if this practice helps you learn something new. Notice whether you develop a better relationship with the person you're talking with. If you try this with several people, you might find yourself laughing in delight as you realize how many unique ways there are to be human.

We have the opportunity many times a day, every day, to be the one who listens to others, curious rather than certain. But the greatest benefit of all is that listening moves us closer. When we listen with less judgment, we always develop better relationships with each other. It's not differences that divide us. It's our judgments about each other that do. Curiosity and good listening bring us back together.

Sometimes we hesitate to listen for differences because we don't want to change. We're comfortable with our lives, and if we listened to anyone who raised questions, we'd have to get engaged in changing things. If we don't listen, things can stay as they are and we won't have to expend any energy. But most of us do see things in our lives or in the world that we would like to be different. If that's true, we have to listen more, not less. And we have to be willing to move into the very uncomfortable place of uncertainty.

We can't be creative if we refuse to be confused. Change always starts with confusion; cherished interpretations must dissolve to make way for the new. Of course, it's scary to give up what we know, but the abyss is where newness lives. Great ideas and inventions miraculously appear in the space of not knowing. If we can move through the fear and enter the abyss, we are rewarded greatly. We rediscover we're creative.

As the world grows more strange and puzzling and difficult, I don't believe most of us want to keep struggling through it alone. I can't know what to do from my own narrow perspective. I know I need a better understanding of what's going on. I want to sit down with you and talk about all the frightening and hopeful things I observe, and listen to what frightens you and gives you hope. I need new ideas and solutions for the problems I care about. I know I need to talk to you to discover those. I need to learn to value your perspective, and I want you to value mine. I expect to be disturbed by what I hear from you. I know we don't have to agree with each other in order to think well together. There is no need for us to be joined at the head. We are joined by our human hearts.

Double-Entry Journal

This process allows you to interact with a text by taking notes, then making notes.

Directions: Reread the essay from Margaret Wheatley's book. Think about what her ideas might mean to a teacher. On the left side of this page, record Wheatley's words that challenge, confuse, or resonate with your thinking about being a teacher in a diverse classroom. On the right side, respond to your notes by making connections to your thinking, questions, other texts, thoughts, and ideas.

Notes/quotes from the text	Your response to the notes/quotes
Ex: We weren't trained to admit we don't know.	*Teachers aren't hired for this, either. The world rewards assertions, not uncertainty. How can I change that for myself? For students?*

Quotation/sentence from text

Response/reflection

1.

1.

Award Acceptance/Toast

Strategy 11

Future Selves, Present Goals

RATIONALE

As you move from examining your own identity to examination of your public, professional identity, goal setting offers another vehicle for merging your personal and professional identities. The "Award Acceptance/Toast" strategy asks you to imagine what you would like to be remembered for as an educator in the form of a first-person thank you speech or as the master of ceremonies addressing a crowd assembled to honor you. "Imagining future selves" moves you from asking, "Who am I?" in an egocentric sense to asking, "Who am I as a teacher?" and "What do I want my students to remember about me and the classroom ecosystem we shared?" From the ecosystem perspective, this strategy will help you to learn more about your classmates and get to know them in new ways. It builds community, and it will help you to consider aspects of your emerging professional life in relation to your future students.

NOTE TO INSTRUCTORS

If the excerpt included in the step-by-step instructions is not sufficient to get your students started, you may want to download a complete student sample of the "Toast" strategy from the companion website (**http://www.sagepub.com/buckelew**) to share.

STEP-BY-STEP INSTRUCTIONS

1. Imagine a day on which you are being honored at an award banquet for your achievements in education. What do you want to be remembered for? Categories might include specific lessons or content, extracurricular activities, or general and specific contributions to the field of education. Choose first person or third person to write your toast or acceptance speech, and remember to use substantive and illustrative details. Have fun with it—be lofty, imagine big!

Here is an excerpt from one of Mary's students, Sophia, who chose to write a toast to herself:

> Fellow educators, thank you for coming this evening. It is wonderful to see such a turnout, but not surprising since we are here to honor a colleague who is loved and respected by all—someone who has made so many contributions to the field of education that they are far too numerous to mention. But let me share just a few of her accomplishments in her long and rewarding career as a 10th-grade teacher. Sophia Lopez began teaching 25 years ago in an urban setting in East LA. She was excited to teach in East LA because it's where she grew up. Many of us know the challenges that she faced as a new teacher in those times, but she being the passionate activist that she is knew that she could make a difference. One of her first accomplishments was to contact businesses in the area and secure enough funding so that her students could actually have books of their own—books that they could take home, Biology and Earth Science books that inspired them. This 25-year-old program, Community Connections: Books for a Better Life for All—is still going on today—thanks to Sophia's continued efforts. Please hold the applause! Her next accomplishment—and I know Sophia does not want to be the center of attention, I can see her blushing—but her next accomplishment, the Community Connections: Gardening for Science Self-Sufficiency project is 15 years old and still going strong. As our biology, earth science, and environmental science teacher, Sophia dreamed that her students would be able to see the real-life applications of what she was teaching and so, through her determination and diligence, she once again convinced our business community to help her to realize a dream for the good of all. In fact, the food we're eating tonight came directly . .
> I think you get the idea.

2. Write a draft of your toast or award acceptance speech.

3. Pair-share: Tell each other what stood out for you as the listener.

4. Whole class: Share some of the speeches with your class.

5. Place in your professional portfolio.

LOOKING BACK/LOOKING AHEAD

In a few sentences, reflect upon your experience with this strategy. What did you notice? What surprised you? Explain how you might use this strategy in your future classroom.

_____

_____

_____

_____

_____

CONTENT-AREA EXTENSIONS

Cross-Curricular: Using substantive and illustrative detail from the pertinent discipline area, write a testimonial in first or third person regarding why you (or a historical figure) should be remembered as a person who was top in his or her field: science, math, kinesiology, history, psychology, and so on.

ADDITIONAL APPLICATION

This strategy helps new teachers think about their future goals while also learning more about their colleagues. It helps veteran teachers get to know each other in new ways. For both groups, it builds community and it often rejuvenates the group.

SECTION II

Multicultural Awareness and Intercultural Interaction

As in naturally occurring ecosystems, the nature and quality of human relationships may shift in more or less productive ways. Each strategy in this section is designed to foreground the connectedness and interactions in the classroom ecosystem, making participants aware of both productive and counterproductive behavior. Each one also requires that students see themselves and each other as individuals, who belong to groups but are not defined by any associated stereotypes (see Figure II.1).

Figure II.1   The Individual in the Classroom

This is the individual in the classroom having experiences or transactions that enter his or her linguistic/experiential reservoir where they encounter, mix, or conflict with what's already there from home and the community. Arrows are double-headed because the individual has to deal with input and output.

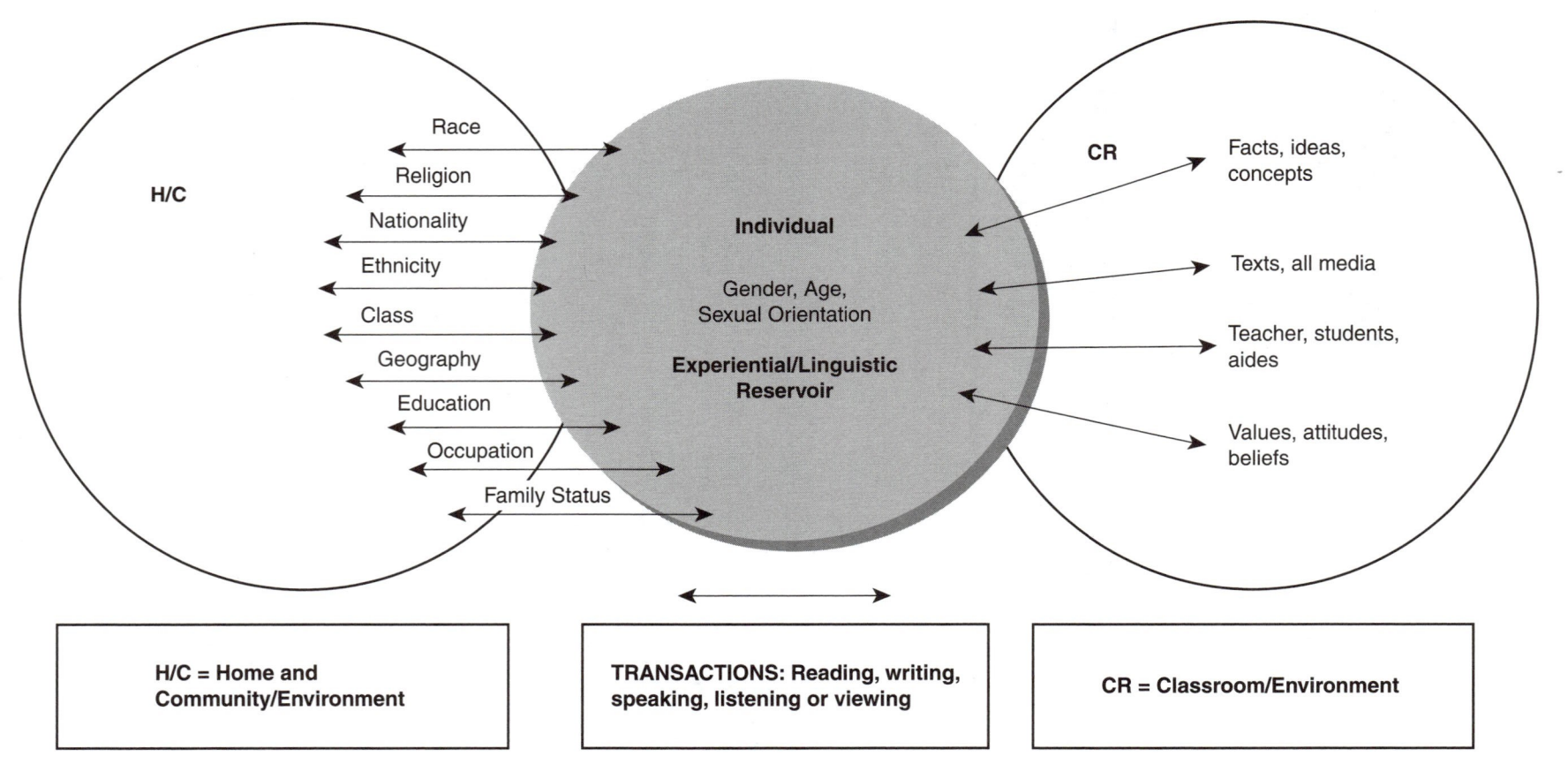

Shared Language and Guidelines

Creating a Classroom Culture of Respect

Strategy 12

Misconceptions may abound in a diverse classroom setting. A seemingly small example from Mary's own classroom illustrates how misconceptions arise and how a negative perception of a classmate or student might be shaped by something as inconsequential as a yawn. In the midst of a mini-lesson in a rather small but very diverse class of 20 high school students, Mary was greeted by one of the most enthusiastic yawns she'd ever encountered in a classroom setting. Not only was it a robust yawn, but the young man did not cover his mouth. Mary politely reminded him that one usually covers one's mouth when yawning. The student looked confused, so Mary explained that in the culture and context of a typical U.S. classroom, such a yawn without at least a hand over the mouth might be construed as rude. At least, that's what she'd been taught. He apologized and explained he did not realize this was the case. Another student said she had never heard that one should cover one's mouth either. The student who had yawned shyly explained his grandmother had told him that yawning was just the soul's way of escaping the body for awhile to fly with the gods. Mary thanked him for educating the class on another perspective regarding yawns. A discussion on culture and context ensued.

It is just these kinds of differing perceptions that cause teachers and students alike to judge each other unfairly. A major goal in the social ecosystem of the classroom, then, is to promote understanding in order to create a community of learners. At the most basic level, building community requires that all students comprehend the guidelines for classroom interaction. In the diverse classroom, laying the foundation for this means understanding the home, culture, and community rules (written and unwritten) that students—and teachers—bring. In a diverse classroom, finding connections and distinctions between the classroom guidelines and the rules of interaction in students' lives outside of the classroom ecosystem frames the discussion and creation of classroom guidelines of respect and interaction.

In the context of the ecosystem, the following strategy covers just one way of creating a safe and stable classroom in which everyone thrives. It starts you on the path toward thinking about your future classroom and how you will build and maintain respect for all individuals within the classroom ecosystem.

Note to Instructor

Because respect is such a crucial ingredient in any classroom ecosystem, this is one of the first activities that you may want to do with your students. Establishing a common language of respect is invaluable, especially when discussing controversial issues such as stereotypes, race, class, gender, and multicultural issues. Coming to a shared understanding of classroom guidelines and a shared language of respect before having controversial discussions will benefit the classroom ecosystem by making visible what respect looks, sounds, and feels like in the classroom community.

Step-by-Step Instructions

1. Brainstorm general definition of "respect."

2. Divide a notebook page into four columns or quarters.

3. Label the four columns as follows: Column 1: Respect at Home; Column 2: Respect at School; Column 3: Respect in Community; Column 4: Respect in the Classroom.

4. List signs of respect from your life at home, at school, and in the community in which you live. For example, here is a brief list from one of our students. School: be on time, be prepared; Home: take off shoes upon entering the house, greet mother, aunt upon entering house; Community: greet someone with a firm hand-shake, do not look stranger or person of power directly in the eyes when speaking to him or her.

5. Pair-share (or discuss in small groups) your own list with a classmate you do not know. Introduce and discuss your individual examples and make connections among the signs of respect from your home, school, and community and how these translate or don't translate to other settings or contexts.

   For example, Mary's family of origin attended a Roman Catholic church every Sunday when she was a child. She remembers that the women and girls had to wear head coverings as a sign of respect, but the men and boys had to remove their hats for the very same reason. This carried over to other settings, as well. It was rude for men to wear hats inside any building. To this day, if Mary sees a man with a hat on inside a building, she must remind herself that it isn't necessarily rude in all cultures for men to wear hats indoors, and she had to decide how to approach the hat issue in her own classroom. Eventually, the school in which she taught ruled that hats would not be allowed for myriad reasons.

6. Decide and list (in pairs or small groups) 4–5 guidelines for respect that can be used in the class in which you are using this book. List in Column 4—e.g., silence technology or switch technology to vibrate mode.

7. Whole-class discussion: Share ways in which respect is shown in different environments or ecosystems. How might the rules from home play out in other settings? How might the rules of respect from home work for you? Work against you? Discuss commonalities and differences. Share anecdotes about the translation of certain signs of respect from one ecosystem to the next (home, school, community).

8. Whole-class discussion: Decide on 4–5 guidelines for "Respect" in classroom interactions. Also decide on strategies and consequences for working with students/peers who forget or ignore the guidelines of respect for classroom interaction.

   In Mary's high school classroom, the students agreed that the mantra "poise, dignity, and grace" would be directed at any student who was disrupting the learning environment, and would serve as the first reminder to a student that he or she was interfering with the equilibrium of the classroom ecosystem. For example, if one student interrupted another, Mary or another student might say, "Please have poise, dignity, and grace, John." This mantra became second nature for everyone, and it was a direct but gentle way of reminding students that their behavior was interfering with the learning of others. If the behavior was repeated, students agreed upon consequences that seemed fair and just.

9. Record and display guidelines for respect, strategies, and consequences for infractions on the board or on a poster-size Post-it.

LOOKING BACK/LOOKING AHEAD

Write about your experience with this strategy—the process, product, and discussions. How might you use the strategy "Creating a Classroom Culture of Respect" in your own class?

_____

_____

_____

_____

_____

CONTENT-AREA EXTENSIONS

Language Arts/ESL/Foreign Languages: The "Respect" strategy can be included in a lesson on abstract nouns, verbs, and so forth (parts of speech).

ADDITIONAL APPLICATION

This strategy affords new teachers and veteran teachers the opportunity to examine and discuss their classroom rules/guidelines and the school rules in light of their own diverse student populations and the rules of interaction that their students bring to the classroom and building. New and veteran teachers can consider how visible and clear the classroom and school rules of interaction are for their students.

Strategy 13

Just Because*

*We borrowed the "Just Because" strategy from our colleague Michele Curay-Cramer. Michele could not remember from whom she had borrowed it. Our student, Lauren Segarra, developed the graphic organizer for her seventh graders (included at end of strategy).

RATIONALE

Assumptions based on first impressions often lead to unfair stereotypes and judgments about groups and individuals. In the context of the classroom ecosystem, stereotyping leads to misconceptions that may inhibit community building or prevent collaboration among students. Further, if the teacher also sees his or her students through the lenses of stereotypes, he or she may, unknowingly, impose potentially destructive limitations on the curriculum and content offered to groups or individual students. Examining such first-impression stereotypes in this strategy will help you and your classmates understand how easy it is to stereotype and how stereotypes tend to be imprecise and misleading. This strategy is an extension of the final activities in Section I, which help you analyze how seeing beyond the surface meaning of a piece of literature, the exterior of an object, or the look of a painting fosters ways of seeing that can assist you as a future teacher in creating a classroom ecosystem that honors diversity and uses it to its fullest potential.

NOTE TO INSTRUCTOR

In this strategy, you may want to suggest that students think of roles they play in their daily lives that they know may have negative connotations (see graphic organizer and sample poems at end of strategy).

After students complete the activities below, we urge you to show the video *Chimamanda Adichie: The Danger of a Single Story* (www.ted.com/talks/chimamanda_adichie_the_danger_of_a_single_story.html). Discuss Adichie's message with your students in light of their "Just Because" poems and their future classrooms. We have found this video and the ensuing discussions to have a profound effect on students.

STEP-BY-STEP INSTRUCTIONS

1. If you already identified a list of roles in Section I, Strategy 1, "My Life as a _____," revisit it now, and skip to Step 3. If you did not do this strategy as a class, move on to Step 2 below.

2. Brainstorm the different roles that you play on a daily basis. For instance, one of Mary's students listed the following items: music lover, skateboarder, student, tattoo artist, son, brother, reader, tennis player, shopper, hacky sack player. Brainstorm your own roles.

3. Select one role and use the graphic organizer provided at the end of this strategy to brainstorm the "just because" for different stereotypes associated with the role.

4. Using the following stems, compose your own "Just Because" poem. Use the samples at the end of this strategy as models.
   "Just because I am _____
   Doesn't mean _____.""

5. Pair-share with a classmate. Discuss experiences you have had with stereotyping because of one or more of the roles you wrote about.

6. Whole-class discussion: Share poems with classmates and discuss the impact of stereotypes in your own lives as well as the potential impact in your future classrooms.

7. Place poem in your professional portfolio.

LOOKING BACK/LOOKING AHEAD

Write about your experience with this strategy—the process, product, and discussions. How might you use the "Just Because" poem in your own class?

_____

_____

_____

_____

_____

CONTENT-AREA EXTENSIONS

Language Arts/History/Science/Math: This strategy provides another lens for reading literature and history texts, among others. Students can examine characters, historical figures, scientific terminology, or math theorems through the "Just Because" lens.

ADDITIONAL APPLICATION

This strategy serves the same purpose with any group of teachers. It gives both new and veteran teachers a chance to examine their assumptions in light of themselves, their colleagues, and their own students.

Name _____   Date _____

Directions:

1. Select one role from the "My life as a _____" Strategy.

2. Brainstorm stereotypes regarding this role.

3. See student sample.

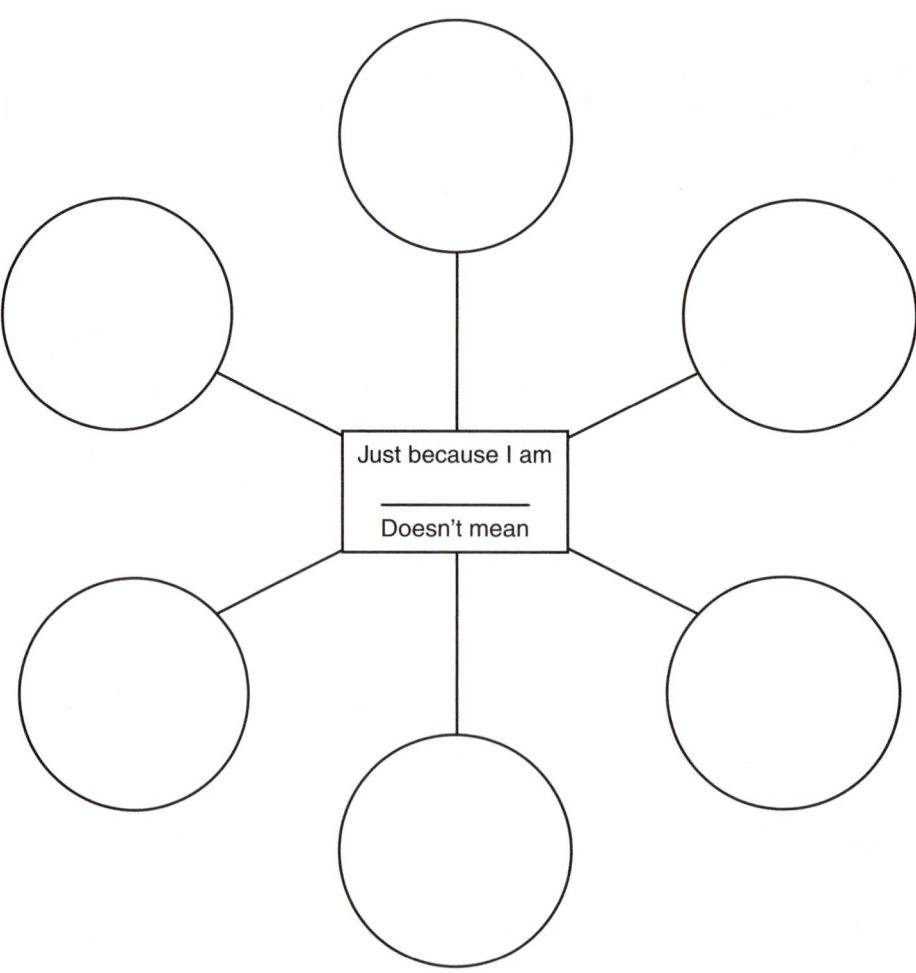

Name _____   Date _____

Directions:

1. Select one role from the "My life as a _____" Strategy.

2. Brainstorm stereotypes regarding this role.

3. See student sample.

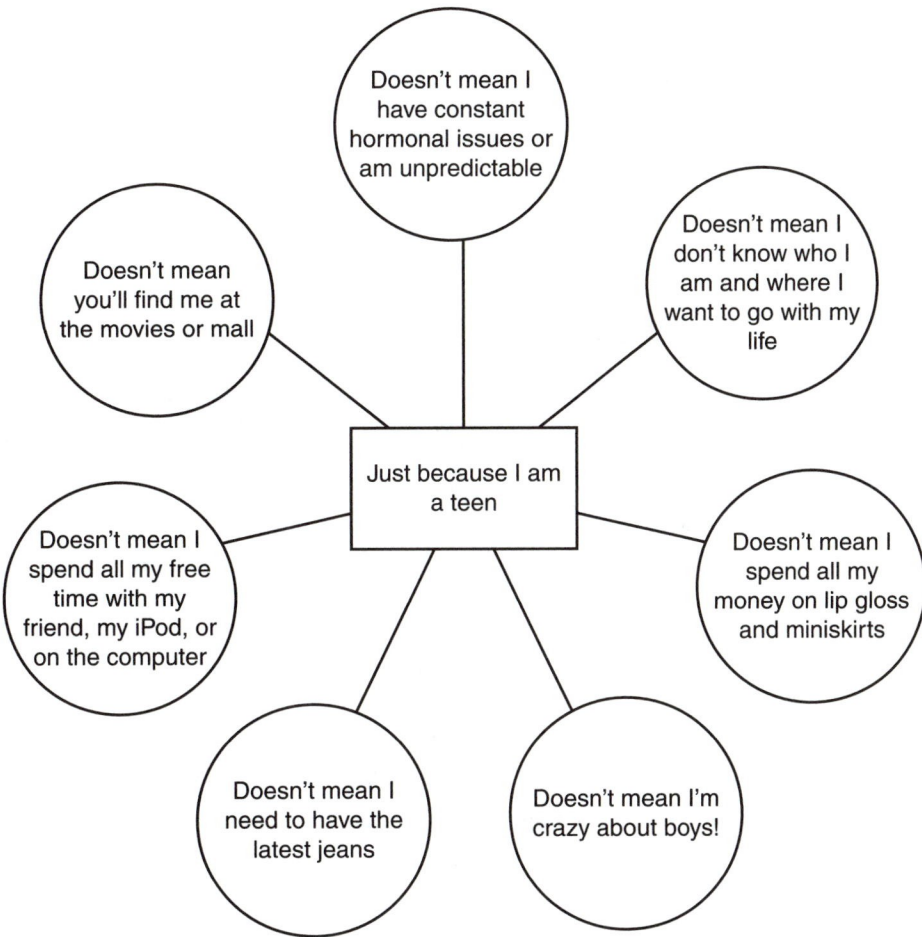

"Just Because" Poem Samples

Just because I'm a skateboarder
Doesn't mean I don't like golf.
Just because I'm a skateboarder
Doesn't mean "Dude" is what I call my dad.
Just because I'm a skateboarder
Doesn't mean I don't read Steinbeck.
Just because I'm a skateboarder
Doesn't mean I deface public property.

Just because I'm a teen
Doesn't mean I am unpredictable

Just because I'm a teen
Doesn't mean I don't know where I want to go with my life

Just because I'm a teen
Doesn't mean I need to have the latest jeans or
spend all my money on lip gloss and mini skirts

Just because I'm a teen
Doesn't mean I am crazy about boys

Just because I'm a teen
Doesn't mean I spend all my time at the movies or mall and
spend my free time with my friends, iPod, or computer
Just because I'm a teen

A-List/B-List

Getting Beyond Stereotypes

Strategy 14

The "cultures" most often identified with the term *multicultural* are broad, unilateral categories. We call these the A-list: **race, ethnicity, religion, gender,** and **nationality.** Though these headings yield a variety of combinations (e.g., African American man, Jewish American woman, Italian Catholic; Iraqi Muslim), it is these combinations that produce the most enduring stereotypes, as seen everywhere from political cartoons to airport security to debates about police profiling.

Not only are these categories often counterproductive, but they are also insufficient for understanding the truly complex identity of *every* person in a classroom community. This is particularly important in apparently homogeneous settings, where everyone seems to look alike and where white, Anglo-Saxon, Protestant students often complain, "We have no culture," believing that "this multicultural stuff is all about them, not us."

Combining the A-list with the B-list addresses both these problems. First, it precludes the superficial labeling that leads to stereotyping. The B-list categories—**class, age, geography, education, occupation, family status,** and **sexual orientation**—differentiate each individual from the broad A-list groups to which they belong. Second, it offers ways into a positive personal understanding of multiculturalism for even the most seemingly generic students.

For example, Andrea's A-list looks like this: white, Jewish, American, woman. That distinguishes her from Mary only to the extent that she is Jewish while Mary is Catholic. Otherwise, they seem identical.

Andrea's B-list, however, reveals that she is a leading-edge baby boomer, who grew up in New York City, the only child of a doctor father and stay-at-home mother. She went to a small, eastern liberal arts college and has lived in Pennsylvania for almost her entire adult life. She is divorced and remarried with one son, three stepchildren, and ten grandchildren. That makes her a mother, stepmother, and grandmother in addition to being a former high school English teacher and now an English professor.

Mary's B-list reveals significant differences. She was born nine years after Andrea, and she is the oldest of ten children born to an Italian Catholic father and British, converted Catholic mother. Though raised in upstate New York, she went to the University of New Mexico and spent the first 25 years of her adult life in Albuquerque. She is widowed and remarried, with one daughter, who is currently in college, and one son, who is in the military. She, too, is a former high school English teacher and now an English professor.

So, while Mary and Andrea seem nearly identical in A-list terms, their identities—and relationship—are clearly enriched by B-list descriptors. Conversely, the same happens when pairs with significant A-list differences allow their B-list features to connect them in unexpected ways.

This strategy is also a prelude to developing critical consciousness about the power of the invisible in everyone's life and relationships with others. Making the unseen visible—putting it into words—is the first step toward asking questions about what else is not known.

Step-by-Step Instructions

1. Write down your A-list identities.

2. Pair-share: To what extent do your A-list descriptors encompass who you are? Which one is the noun and which the adjectives? Do your descriptors always stay in those positions? When might you change that? (For example, sometimes Andrea is a Jewish American woman. Other times, she's an American Jew who happens to be a woman.)

3. Write down your B-list descriptors.

4. Pair-share: What difference did the B-list make in your ability to self-identify? When you apply for your first teaching position, what else might you want prospective employers to know about you? If you went on match.com, what else would you want to know about a prospective date—or want a prospective date to know about you?

5. Develop a Venn diagram for you and your partner, using your A-list/B-list descriptors. What happens when you do this?

6. Whole-class discussion: How might thinking in A-list/B-list terms inform who you see in your classroom? How you respond to students who seem unlike you? To parents who seem unlike you?

7. Put your lists and Venn diagram in your professional portfolio.

Looking Back/Looking Ahead

What was it like to do this strategy? How might you use "A-list/B-list: Getting Beyond Stereotypes" in your own classroom?

_____

_____

_____

_____

_____

CONTENT-AREA EXTENSIONS

Language Arts: This strategy helps students find ways into multicultural literature. Instead of doing the Venn diagram with classmates, students can find connections to literary characters that seem significantly different from themselves.

Social Studies: This strategy can be modified to focus on cultures, rather than individuals, resulting in Venn diagrams that compare the culture in which students live with a culture they are studying.

Foreign Language: This strategy can help students connect with their counterparts who speak another language or connect their culture with the culture where the language is spoken.

ADDITIONAL APPLICATION

This strategy serves the same anti-stereotyping purpose with any group of teachers. New teachers can consider what it reveals about their student-teaching experiences. What would the Venn diagram look like with them on one side and their cooperating teacher on the other? A student on the other?

Veteran teachers can consider how it changes their approach to new classes. Both new and veteran teachers can consider how it affects their views of current students, parents, or colleagues. The strategy also helps build community among school, department, or grade-level groups.

Talking Back

Found and Two-Voice Poetry

Strategy 15

RATIONALE

A major goal of multicultural and intercultural education is to help students hear what others have to say, ideally in a way that no one feels preached at, put down, or punished. This is particularly important when male or white or Christian or middle-class students are confronted with minority or female voices that seem angry *at them*. Few people respond constructively to being scolded, so diatribes, even monologues, can be counterproductive when it comes to hearing and understanding each other. These kinds of lectures create a disequilibrium that makes everyone uncomfortable and fosters hard feelings that get in the way of learning.

This strategy facilitates dialogue instead. It asks you to respond to texts, so no one feels lectured and no one goes unheard. It can be done in a variety of ways, using voices from inside and outside the classroom.

It uses poetry for four reasons: (1) Poetry is generally succinct, to the point, and short; (2) poetry provides a simple format that can sound like speech; (3) poetry is flexible, i.e., words and phrases can be organized in whatever way you choose; and (4) poetry can be "found" in everything you read, including textbooks, magazines, newspapers, and websites.

Finding poetry in what you read is the first step. Here is an example from Gollnick and Chinn's *Multicultural Education in a Pluralistic Society* (2008). The first paragraph in a section headed "Race" reads as follows:

Are racial groups also ethnic groups? In the United States, many people use the two terms interchangeably. Racial groups include many ethnic groups, and ethnic groups may include members of more than one racial group. Race is a concept that was developed by physical anthropologists to describe the physical characteristics of people in the world more than a century ago—a practice that has now been discredited. It is not a stable category for organizing and differentiating people. Instead, it is a social-historical concept dependent on society's perception that differences exist and that these differences are important. Some theorists suggest that race, as used in the United States, is equivalent to **caste** in other countries. Throughout U.S. history, racial identification has been used by policymakers and much of the population to classify groups of people as inferior or superior to other racial groups, resulting in discrimination and inequality against persons of color. (p. 59, emphasis original)

52

Here is a poem that can be "found" in this paragraph:

RACE

A concept developed by anthropologists
To describe physical characteristics
More than a century ago
Now discredited.

Instead, a social-historical concept
Dependent on perception
That differences are important.

Used to classify groups of people
As inferior or superior.

Resulting in discrimination
And inequality
Against persons of color.

If a white student, for example, composed this found poem, it could become one voice to which he or she can talk back, creating a two-voice poem like the one below. The found poem is on the left; the student's response is on the right, in italics:

RACE

A concept developed by anthropologists
To describe physical characteristics
More than a century ago
Now discredited.

19ᵗʰ century thinking couldn't survive
21ˢᵗ century consciousness.

Instead, a social historical concept
Dependent on perception
That differences are important.

Some differences are important.
Not skin color, hair texture,
nose shape, lip size.

Used to classify groups of people
As inferior or superior

Works for me. Makes my life easier.

Resulting in discrimination
And inequality
Against persons of color.

Not so great for my black roommate.

Students of color may have very different responses to the same paragraph, as may other white students.

STEP-BY-STEP INSTRUCTIONS

FOUND POETRY

1. Identify a text to which you might "talk back." It can be in first or third person, fact or fiction, current or historical. Possible sources include textbooks, literature, the Internet, and even the daily newspaper. Children's literature is also a wonderful source.

2. Highlight/underline words, phrases, or sentences that capture events or ideas important in that text.

3. On a separate piece of paper, arrange those selected portions into free-form poems that express the main ideas of the text.

TWO-VOICE POEMS

1. Identify lines in your found poem about which you have something to say. You can agree, disagree, compare/contrast, or simply comment.

2. "Talk back" to the voice in your found poem, writing lines in response to that text. These lines may alternate with the found voice or, in instances where you feel the same way, a single line can be said by both, creating a choral effect.

3. Pair-share: Working with a partner, practice reading your two-voice poems aloud. You will each read your partner's found voice.

4. When you have practiced enough to read smoothly, present your two-voice poems orally to the class.

5. Whole-class discussion: What was it like to hear and to write these dialogues, in terms of both what you felt and what you learned?

6. Place your poem in your professional portfolio.

LOOKING BACK/LOOKING AHEAD

What was it like to do this strategy? How might you use "Found and Two-Voice Poetry" in your own classroom?

_____

_____

_____

_____

_____

CONTENT-AREA EXTENSIONS

Language Arts: When reading multicultural literature, found poems can be in the voice of a character that is like or unlike the reader. The two-voice poem then becomes a conversation between a character from the text and the student.

Social Studies and Foreign Language: Students can find their found poems in any literature or textbook they use in their classes.

ADDITIONAL APPLICATION

New and veteran teachers can find the voices for their found poems in their daily lives at school. Possible sources include school newspapers, daily announcements, overheard conversations between students or colleagues, the district website, or texts they are currently using in their classes.

SUGGESTION BOX

Nonfiction children's literature is an excellent source of texts for this strategy. Consider books like *Passage to Freedom: The Sugihara Story,* by Ken Mochizuki; *Yours for Justice, Ida B. Wells,* by Philip Dray; or *Rachel: The Story of Rachel Carson,* by Amy Ehrlich.

Try this strategy with other texts. Newspapers, magazines, and websites often present voices to which you might want to "talk back." Look particularly for discussions of "hot topics" like don't ask/don't tell, school bussing, Ebonics, service learning, or the achievement gap. Just make sure it's something about which you have something to say.

Finding Ways In

Translating Others' Experiences

Strategy 16

RATIONALE

This is a variation on Strategy 5, "Professional Identity Collage," that focuses on one voice at a time. The voices can be found in literature, biography, memoir, film, blogs, or any other text in which people describe or enact what it means to be who they are, where they are. Translating these experiences to reflect your own experiences requires that you find connections between your life, here and now, and others' lives in other places or times, in other communities of all kinds. Translations can be done from one time period to another; one country to another; one gender, race, or ethnicity to another; or from any combination of these.

For example, Jamaica Kincaid's one-page short story, "Girl" (1991), is in the voice of a mother giving instructions to her daughter. The instructions range from "Wash the white clothes on Monday" to "Don't squat down to play marbles." Mixed in with such clear do's and don'ts are warnings to "walk like a lady and not like the slut you are so bent on becoming." It is evident from some of the tasks and some of the vocabulary that this mother–daughter pair does not live in the United States. The idea of a mother instructing her daughter is universal, however, and can be "translated" by changing time and place to a 21st-century American mother instructing her daughter.

Similarly, the excerpt from Tim O'Brien's *The Things They Carried* (1998) illustrates that while all soldiers may look alike with their nearly identical haircuts, uniforms, and ordered movements, the things they carry into battle go beyond general-issue standardization, identifying them as unique individuals within the homogenized ranks. While O'Brien's men are Vietnam-era soldiers, the idea of individuals in any standardized group finding ways to self-identify applies not only to those who wear uniforms (e.g., private, parochial, and even some public school students; marching band or athletic team members), but to any categorized groups (e.g., seventh-grade boys, student council officers, sorority sisters).

Because it is based on similarity, this strategy emphasizes the shared aspects of human experience and makes the differences be the details and the functions of time, place, and heredity rather than individual preference.

STEP-BY-STEP INSTRUCTIONS

1. Read "Girl," by Jamaica Kincaid, and the excerpt from *The Things They Carried,* by Tim O'Brien, found after this strategy.

2. Read the sample translations of "Girl" and *The Things They Carried,* found after this strategy.

3. Working with a partner, identify settings (time, place, and particular culture) into which you can translate whichever text you choose or are assigned.

4. Write (one copy of) your actual translation.

5. With your partner, join two other pairs who used the same starting text to form a small group of six students. Read aloud each of the (three) translations. Take notes on similarities and differences as you listen.

6. Whole-class discussion: Everyone in your group started with the same text. How do you explain the similarities and differences in your group's translations? Where did they come from?

7. Print out or photocopy your translation so both you and your partner can put one in your professional portfolio.

LOOKING BACK/LOOKING AHEAD

What was it like to do this strategy? How might you use "Finding Ways In: Translating Others' Experiences" in your own classroom?

_____

_____

_____

_____

_____

CONTENT-AREA EXTENSIONS

Language Arts: Students can do any of the kinds of translations described in the Rationale section of this strategy, translating literary characters' lives into their own. They can also translate from one genre to another, e.g., writing the newspaper article or poem or blog version of an event in whatever literature they're reading.

Social Studies: Students can do third-person translations of activities or events over time, e.g., warfare then and now, presidential campaigns then and now, economic development then and now.

ADDITIONAL APPLICATION

The only difference in doing this strategy with new or veteran teachers may be the initial texts chosen for translation. It may be most useful to choose texts describing some form of education, e.g., parents raising children (like the Kincaid piece), religious sermons, or excerpts from teacher or student memoirs.

SUGGESTION BOX

Children's literature is a wonderful source of possible texts for this strategy. Consider *When I Was Young in the Mountains, Appalachia,* or *The Relatives Came,* all by Cynthia Rylant; *Aunt Flossie's Hats (and Crab Cakes Later),* by Elizabeth Fitzgerald Howard; or *More Than Anything Else,* by Marie Bradby.

GIRL

By Jamaica Kincaid

Wash the white clothes on Monday and put them on the stone heap; wash the color clothes on Tuesday and put them on the clothesline to dry; don't walk barehead in the hot sun; cook pumpkin fritters in very hot sweet oil; soak your little cloths right after you take them off; when buying cotton to make yourself a nice blouse, be sure that it doesn't have gum on it, because that way it won't hold up well after a wash; soak salt fish overnight before you cook it; is it true that you sing benna in Sunday school?; always eat your food in such a way that it won't turn someone else's stomach; on Sundays try to walk like a lady and not like the slut you are so bent on becoming; don't sing benna in Sunday school; you mustn't speak to wharf-rat boys, not even to give directions; don't eat fruits on the street—flies will follow you; *but I don't sing benna on Sundays at all and never in Sunday school;* this is how to sew a button; this is how to make a buttonhole for the button you have just sewed on; this is how to hem a dress when you see the hem coming down and so to prevent yourself from looking like the slut I know you are so bent on becoming; this is how you iron your father's khaki shirt so that it doesn't have a crease; this is how you iron your father's khaki pants so that they don't have a crease; this is how you grow okra—far from the house, because okra tree harbors red ants; when you are growing dasheen, make sure it gets plenty of water or else it makes your throat itch when you are eating it; this is how you sweep the corner; this is how you sweep the whole house; this is how you sweep a yard; this is how you smile to someone you don't like too much; this is how you smile to someone you don't like at all; this is how you smile to someone you like completely; this is how you set a table for tea; this is how you set a table for dinner; this is how you set a table for dinner with an important guest; this is how you set a table for lunch; this is how you set a table for breakfast; this is how to behave in the presence of men who don't know you very well, and this way they won't recognize immediately the slut I have warned you against becoming; be sure to wash every day, even if it is with your own spit; don't squat down to play marbles—you are not a boy, you know; don't pick people's flowers—you might catch something; don't throw stones at blackbirds, because it might not be a blackbird at all; this is how to make a bread pudding; this is how to make doukona; this is how to make pepper pot; this is how to make a good medicine for a cold; this is how to make a good medicine to throw away a child before it even becomes a child; this is how to catch a fish; this is how to throw back a fish you don't like, and that way something bad won't fall on you; this is how to bully a man; this is how a man bullies you; this is how to love a man, and if this doesn't work there are other ways, and if they don't work don't feel too bad about giving up; this is how to spit up in the air if you feel like it, and this is how to move quick so that it doesn't fall on you; this is how to make ends meet; always squeeze bread to make sure it's fresh; *but what if the baker won't let me feel the bread?;* you mean to say that after all you are really going to be the kind of woman who the baker won't let near the bread?

THE THINGS THEY CARRIED

By Tim O'Brien

The things they carried were largely determined by necessity. Among the necessities or near-necessities were P-38 can openers, pocket knives, heat tabs, wristwatches, dog tags, mosquito repellent, chewing gum, candy, cigarettes, salt tablets, packets of Kool-Aid, lighters, matches, sewing kits, Military Payment Certificates, C rations, and two or three canteens of water. Together, these items weighed between 15 and 20 pounds, depending upon a man's habits or rate of metabolism. Henry Dobbins, who was a big man, carried extra rations; he was especially fond of canned peaches in heavy syrup over pound cake. Dave Jensen, who practices field hygiene, carried a toothbrush, dental floss, and several hotel-sized bars of soap he'd stolen on R&R in Sydney, Australia. Ted Lavender, who was scared, carried tranquilizers until he was shot in the head outside the village of Than Khe in mid-April. By necessity, and because it was SOP, they all carried steel helmets that weighed 5 pounds including the liner and camouflage cover. They carried the standard fatigue jackets and trousers. Very few carried underwear. On their feet they carried jungle boots—2.1 pounds—and Dave Jensen carried three pairs of socks and a can of Dr. Scholl's foot powder as a precaution against trench foot. Until he was shot, Ted Lavender carried 6 or 7 ounces of premium dope, which for him was a necessity. Mitchell Sanders, the RTO, carried condoms. Norman Bowker carried a diary. Rat Kiley carried comic books. Kiowa, a devout Baptist, carried an illustrated New Testament that had been presented to him by his father, who taught Sunday school in Oklahoma City, Oklahoma. As a hedge against bad times, however, Kiowa also carried his grandmother's distrust of the white man, his grandfather's old hunting hatchet. Necessity dictated. Because the land was mined and booby-trapped, it was SOP for each man to carry a steel-centered, nylon-covered flak jacket, which weighed 6.7 pounds, but which on hot days seemed much heavier. Because you could die so quickly, each man carried at least one large compress bandage, usually in the helmet band for easy access. Because the nights were cold, and because the monsoons were wet, each carried a green plastic poncho that could be used as a raincoat or groundsheet or makeshift tent. With its quilted liner, the poncho weighed almost 2 pounds, but it was worth every ounce. In April, for instance, when Ted Lavender was shot, they used his poncho to wrap him up, then to carry him across the paddy, then to lift him into the chopper that took him away.

SAMPLE TRANSLATIONS

Note: These were written by unmarried, white, middle- and upper-middle-class, female students in the Philadelphia suburbs in 2009. How might they be different written by students with other descriptors?

"GIRL," CIRCA 2010

Get your t-shirts out of the dryer right away so they won't wrinkle. Stay away from McDonald's and all those other fast food places. They'll make you fat. Keep Lean Cuisines in your freezer so you have something safe to eat at home. Eat before you go out on a date. You don't want boys to think you're some kind of pig. Don't let people take your picture when you're drunk. Once they get posted on Facebook or YouTube, you can never live them down. If you get a tattoo, make it small and flirty. Put a butterfly on your ankle. The skin there won't droop so much when you get old. Make sure your Botox doctor knows what he's doing. You don't want lumps instead of wrinkles. Nail wraps can look cheap. You don't want to look cheap, do you? Get a mani and a pedi once a month in the winter, once a week in the summer. OPI is the best [nail] polish. Try "I Am Not a Waitress" or "Keys to My Karma." Go to Sephora before you buy makeup. Try on the colors so you don't look like a clown. Be careful who you hook up with. You don't want to get a bad reputation at school. Work out with a trainer so you will look amazing in a strapless prom dress. Try shopping on eBay. You can find Betsey Johnson and Christian Louboutin for almost nothing. You can find anything you want on the Internet. Just don't give away your personal information. You never know who's lurking.

THE THINGS THEY CARRIED, IN HIGH SCHOOL BACKPACKS

The things they carried were largely determined by necessity. Among the necessities and near necessities of 10th-grade girls were three-ring binders with color-coded dividers for American Literature, American History, 2nd- or 3rd-year French or Spanish, Bio, and Algebra III, which some called "pre-calc" or "trig," and all the 3- 5-pound textbooks that went with them, not to mention paperback novels like *The Scarlet Letter*, which was for class, and *Twilight*, which wasn't. More important to many of them were the iPhones, iPods, Blackberries, and flavored lip gloss stuffed into the small outside pockets for easy access in what they considered spare moments and for especially easy return when a teacher approached in what they did not think were moments to spare.

Allison Soames carried chocolate fudge Power Bars along with her cross-country gear. She spent most afternoons either in the weight room or running through the woods and fields surrounding the high school. Her twin in last name only, Addison Soames, carried designer water along with designer sunglasses and a sketch pad for designing the high-fashion clothes she imagined before, during, and after the elective Art course, which she believed would be her entrée to the world of Project Runway.

Jen Marlowe carried dog-eared copies of Allen Ginsberg's *Howl* and T. S. Eliot's *The Love Song of J. Alfred Prufrock*, inspiration for the poetry always in her head and in purple ink in the third spiral-bound notebook she had filled since September. Jen Armstrong carried a dog-eared copy of *Good News for Modern Man*, inspiration for the intention-driven life she was learning to lead in the high school version of Campus Crusade for Christ.

Deep in an inside pocket, Caroline Bowden carried a Valentine's Day Beanie Baby, the only tangible evidence of her first and only love, the seventh-grade lothario who dumped her for Amanda Adams, the newer, prettier, thinner girl who transferred to their middle school that spring. Next to the Beanie Baby was her Calorie Calculator and a baggie filled with vanilla cream Snack Wells, each providing its own sense of control.

These girls and many more could be seen striding, bouncing, and trudging through the oversized glass doors of Neil Armstrong High School every morning just before the first bell.

Traditional American Axioms

Yours, Mine, or Ours?

- A stitch in time saves nine.

- A rolling stone gathers no moss.

- A bird in the hand is worth two in the bush.

- A penny saved is a penny earned.

Axioms vary from culture to culture. We've included axioms in this strategy that may be familiar to you, but as you navigate the activities in this strategy, you will most likely think of axioms that are specific to your own childhood, culture, and context.

Most Americans learn axioms like these from the time they're in elementary school. Many children may hear axioms first from grandparents or teachers or clergy, trying to "raise them up in the way they should go." To some, they seem like harmless sayings, truisms, or even clichés associated with people like Benjamin Franklin or Daniel Webster or William Shakespeare—all old, all seemingly passé.

This strategy suggests that though such American axioms may be old, they are neither irrelevant nor necessarily harmless. Rather, they shape the thinking of individuals and communities, articulating beliefs handed down as received wisdom, entirely true and unquestioned—even when they create an "us versus them" mind-set, reinforce stereotypes, or directly contradict each other.

Consider these axioms about groups of people who could be of the same family, race, or ethnicity. If *blood is thicker than water* or *the apple doesn't fall far from the tree* or *one bad apple spoils the whole barrel*, it is difficult to not *visit the sins of the fathers on the sons* when another one of "them" walks into your classroom—even if you also believe that *all men are created equal* and *you can't judge a book by its cover.*

Consider these contrary axioms about raising—and perhaps teaching—children:

- Any little boy can grow up to be president.

- All work and no play make Jack a dull boy.

- As the twig is bent, so grows the bough.

- Children should be seen and not heard.

- Do as I say, not as I do.

- Don't speak until you're spoken to.
- Experience is the best teacher.
- Father knows best.
- It takes a village to raise a child.
- Mighty oaks from little acorns grow.
- Spare the rod and spoil the child.
- You can catch more flies with honey than you can with vinegar.
- You can lead a horse to water, but you can't make him drink.

About appearances:

- All that glitters is not gold.
- Beauty is in the eye of the beholder.
- Beauty is only skin deep.
- Be it ever so humble, there's no place like home.
- Pretty is as pretty does.
- A thing of beauty is a joy forever.
- You can't be too thin or too rich.
- You can't judge a book by its cover.

About conflict:

- All's fair in love and war.
- Do unto others as you would have them do unto you.
- Don't get mad; get even.
- Go along to get along.
- Good fences make good neighbors.
- He who hesitates is lost.
- Kill or be killed.
- Live and let live.
- The meek shall inherit the earth.
- Shoot first. Ask questions later.
- Speak softly and carry a big stick.
- Strike while the iron is hot.
- The pen is mightier than the sword.
- Those who live by the gun, die by the gun.
- Turnabout is fair play.
- Turn the other cheek.

- Two wrongs don't make a right.
- You can catch more flies with honey than you can with vinegar.
- You're either for me or against me.

About gender:

- Boys will be boys.
- Frailty, thy name is woman.
- Hell hath no fury like a woman scorned.
- Snips, snails, and puppy dog tails, that's what little boys are made of.
- Sugar and spice and everything nice, that's what little girls are made of.
- The female of the species is deadlier than the male.
- What's good for the goose is good for the gander.
- Woman's work is never done.

About the relationship between individual and community:

- A house divided against itself cannot stand.
- All for one and one for all.
- All men are created equal.
- Every man for himself.
- He who laughs last laughs best.
- Many hands make light work.
- Neither a borrower nor a lender be.
- No man is an island.
- One for all and all for one.
- One good turn deserves another.
- Pull yourself up by your own bootstraps.
- Share and share alike.
- Too many cooks spoil the broth.
- Two heads are better than one.
- We must all hang together or we shall all hang separately.

About winning and losing:

- Don't count your chickens before they hatch.
- Don't cry over spilled milk.
- Every cloud has a silver lining.
- He who laughs last, laughs best.

- If at first you don't succeed, try, try again.

- It's not whether you win or lose, but how you play the game.

- Knowledge is power.

- Money is power.

- Nothing succeeds like success.

- Nothing ventured, nothing gained.

- Only the strong survive.

- To the victor belong the spoils.

- Virtue is its own reward.

- Winning isn't the most important thing; it's the only thing.

How do people who hold these various beliefs raise their children? What values do they hold dear? What do they expect of their schools? Their government? Each other? Understanding the role these axiomatic values, attitudes, and beliefs play in creating cultural coherence—or cultural conflict—helps us understand what may underlie your own and others' behavior, and provides a way to assess whether people are *all talk, no action,* or whether they actually *walk their talk.* Deciding which axioms are truly your own—and our own—creates a basis for positive interaction and a healthy classroom ecosystem.

Step-by-Step Instructions

1. Choose one axiom from the list above to discuss with your partner.

   If someone believes what you've chosen, how would that affect the way that person lives his or her life? List the possible results.

   For example, if someone believes *a stitch in time saves nine,* that person will work to take care of his or her possessions in a timely way. That person won't wait until the car runs out of gas to fill the tank. He or she won't wait until the night before a paper is due to begin writing it. That person will also write down his or her parents' birthdays so as not to have to make up for forgetting them.

2. Now list the values and possible attitudes of someone with the belief you chose. For example, if someone believes *a stitch in time saves nine,* he or she values planning ahead, taking responsibility, being accountable, being on time, and paying attention to detail. That person may admire someone with those traits and look down on someone who always waits until the last minute and then must scramble to compensate.

3. In a small group of 4–5 students, choose a complete set of themed axioms from the list above.

4. Each of you should choose one of the axioms in the set to analyze the same way you just analyzed the axiom in Steps 1 and 2. In other words, what would someone do who believes the axiom you chose from the group set? What would the person value? Write down your thoughts.

5. Share your axiom analysis with the group and listen to theirs.

6. Discuss these questions: How would the people you just described raise their children? What would those people expect of their children's teachers? How might a teacher respond to those parents who objected to some aspect of his or her teaching or classroom management? How might he or she use axiom awareness to begin addressing the situation?

7. Whole-class discussion: What are the connections between what individual teachers believe, value, and do and what the students—and families—in their classrooms believe, value, and do? How might teachers most effectively deal with what are really conflicts of values and beliefs?

8. Write your personal axiom reflection: (1) What beliefs are most truly your own? How might what you believe affect your professional work and relationships? (2) How will you respond to people—e.g., colleagues, students, or parents—who question what you believe? (3) How might you respond to colleagues, students, administrators, or parents—whose beliefs are different from your own?

9. Place this reflection in your professional portfolio.

LOOKING BACK/LOOKING AHEAD

What was it like to do this strategy? How might you use "Traditional American Axioms: Yours, Mine, or Ours?" in your own classroom?

_____

_____

_____

_____

_____

CONTENT-AREA EXTENSIONS

Language Arts: What axioms articulate the beliefs of and explain conflicts between characters in literature? Express literary themes?

Social Studies: How might cultural axioms clarify historical or political battles?

Foreign Language: What are the axioms of cultures where the language is spoken? How are they phrased in the language?

ADDITIONAL APPLICATION

Both new and veteran teachers can apply this strategy to their actual classrooms, schools, and districts in a variety of ways. They can look at . . .

. . . the words of the district mission statement and the axioms, values, attitudes, and beliefs they reflect. To what extent are the axioms of communities served by the district? How might axiomatic disconnects suggest ways to solve school–community problems?

. . . a recent conflict with a student, a parent, or between two students. What axioms might explain what happened? How might that point toward a solution?

. . . classroom or building rules most often broken. What axiomatic beliefs underlie the rules? What beliefs might motivate the rule breakers? How might awareness of these differences suggest a solution to these problems?

. . . conflicts between colleagues over what or how to teach and discipline students. How might axiomatic differences be causing these conflicts? Suggest resolutions?

. . . any difficult situation through the axiomatic lens. Ask whether the beliefs people seem to hold are actually the beliefs they value. How might enacting their actual beliefs improve the situation?

Processing White Privilege and Examining Racism

Strategy 18

One of the crucial aspects of multicultural teacher education is to "prepare all students to work actively toward structural equality in organizations and institutions" (National Association for Multicultural Education, 2003). The following activities are designed to heighten your awareness regarding the inequities that continue to exist in society and in systems in general. They also give you and your classmates an opportunity to examine your own biases and blind spots, all of which may be detrimental to your future students. The foundation for the strategy is Peggy McIntosh's seminal work, "White Privilege: Unpacking the Invisible Knapsack." Reading this essay and participating in the accompanying activities allows you to examine your own experiences with earned and unearned privilege, racism, and systemic inequities. In light of the classroom ecosystem, this strategy opens the door for having "courageous conversations" to strengthen community in your current classroom and to prepare you to create a safe and equitable classroom environment in the future.

NOTE TO INSTRUCTOR

The heightened awareness of the instructor is key for this strategy, i.e., the instructor should read the accompanying facilitator's guide and the essay "White Privilege"—both found as part of this strategy—before facilitating any of the accompanying activities. While we include step-by-step instructions for this strategy, McIntosh's facilitator's guide below provides a plethora of suggestions that you may want to implement as well. Once students have read the essay and followed the step-by-step instructions, we suggest a whole-class discussion, using the activities and ideas in McIntosh's guide.

You may also want to pair McIntosh's piece with Gloria Yamato's essay "Something About the Subject Makes It Hard to Name" (2004), found at the end of this strategy.

SOME NOTES FOR FACILITATORS ON PRESENTING MY WHITE PRIVILEGE PAPERS

1. My work is not about blame, shame, guilt, or whether one is a "nice person." It's about observing, realizing, thinking systemically and personally. It is about seeing privilege, the "up-side" of oppression and discrimination. It is about unearned advantage, which can also be described as exemption from discrimination.

2. Please do not generalize from my papers. They are about my experience, not about the experiences of all white people in all times and places and circumstances. This qualification is in the paragraph in each paper just before the list begins. If understood, it allays white readers' fears that a paper on privilege will call them racist.

3. Keep "the lists" in their autobiographical contexts. This is a matter of scholarly integrity. It will also increase your effectiveness to be able to say, "This is from just one white woman coming to see she's white in her time and place and workspace. . . . She's writing about herself, not about you."

4. I feel strongly that the work goes best when the facilitator draws on the participants' own personal experiences of advantage and disadvantage, rather than on their opinions. Opinions invite argumentation. Experience invites listening without resisting. Habits of argument work against listening and learning.

5. When exploring privilege, it is useful to use what I have named "serial testimony," a disciplined mode in which each participant gets to respond in turn, uninterrupted, for, say, *one minute,* timed. I call this "the autocratic administration of time in the service of democratic distribution of time." But without rigorous use of a watch or timer, serial testimony can be as undemocratic as any other form of discussion.

6. Understand that every participant has an intricate "politics of location" (Adrienne Rich) within the systems of social power. All people in a workshop or class will have a lifetime of experiences of both empowerment and disempowerment, overwhelming or subtle, within many different systems of power. At the same time all are uniquely individual; no individual is shaped only by their location in systems of power.

7. Co-presentations and panels of people speaking about their experiences one after another can be very effective. I do not usually arrange for "dialogues," since I feel they are often a veiled form of debating and fighting, rather than listening and learning. I avoid "crosstalk" after panels except to allow requests for clarification of what a speaker meant—practicing what Peter Elbow calls The Believing Game.

8. My lists of unearned privileges are not "check lists," questionnaires, or confessional readings.

9. Please draw attention to the specificity of "my sample." I compared my circumstances only with what I knew of the circumstances of my African-American female colleagues in the same building and line of work. This sample is very specific with regard to race, sex, region, location, workplace, vocation, and nation.

10. At the same time it is good to point out the institutional implications of the examples, e.g., in the references to school curricula, the IRS, the police, the media, law, medicine, and business, etc.

11. Invite people to make their own autobiography lists of privilege, for example, about:

Sexual Orientation	Gender	Language
Class	Employment	Nation of Origin
Region	Physical Ability	Parents' relation to education
Religion	Handedness	

12. Be wary of definitions of power and privilege. They lack nuances and complexity.

13. Beware of gym-exercises which position people in only one aspect of their identities, asking them to step forward or backward from a baseline at a given prompt.

14. Avoid self-righteousness or preaching to family and friends about privilege.

15. Explain the word "systemic." Help participants or students to learn what it is to see society systemically, rather than only in terms of individuals making individual choices.

16. Understand why U.S. people, especially White people, have trouble seeing systemically. Explain the myth of meritocracy: that the unit of society is the individual and that whatever one ends up with one must be whatever that individual wanted, worked for, earned, and deserved. This myth, which is one mainstay of capitalist ideology, suppresses knowledge of systemic oppression and especially its "up-side"—systemic privilege.

17. Work to strengthen two intellectual muscles: (a) the ability to see in terms of systems as well as in terms of individuals; (b) the ability to see how systemic discrimination is matched by systemic privilege.

18. Think about the privileges [at] work in schools and universities as making one smarter, not necessarily better. Academic institutions do not claim that making us better is their primary goal.

When I present, or co-present with a person of color, on Privilege Systems, whether or not I am the first to speak, I usually:

- tell how I came to see men's privilege and their obliviousness to it, which made me understand literally my own race privilege and my obliviousness to it, and that "niceness" has nothing to do with it.

- read some examples from my white privilege list, and sometimes read some of my heterosexual privilege list, Christian privilege list, and lists of privilege relative to Asian Americans, Indigenous people, Latino/as, etc

- analyze some of the different misreadings of my paper by white people and people of color.

- raise the question of how I can use unearned advantage to weaken systems of unearned advantage, and why I would want to.

The co-presenter and I take equal time to testify about how we came to see privilege systems in and around us. After this, we use Serial Testimony. We form either circles of five to eight people or pairs of two people to respond in turn, uninterrupted for one minute each, to the following prompts:

Round one: What is one way you've had unearned disadvantage in your life?

Round two: What is one way you've had unearned advantage in your life?

Round three: What is it like for you to sit here and talk about and hear about these experiences of unearned advantage and disadvantage?

Round three is like a debrief in itself. Any further debrief should be on *new* learnings from the exercise. Unfacilitated discussion of the exercise can quickly lead away from experience to generalization and opinions people came into the session with.

Some people "get" the idea of systemic privilege and ask "But what can I do?" My answer is that those in a dominant group can use unearned advantage to weaken systems of unearned advantage. I see white privilege as a bank account that I did not ask for, but that I can choose to spend. People with privilege have far more power than we have been taught to realize under the myth of meritocracy. Participants can brainstorm about how to use unearned assets to share power. Assets may include time, money, leisure, connections, spaces, mobility, security or peace of mind, and may help us to make changes in behavior, such as paying better attention, making associations, intervening, speaking up, asserting and deferring, being alert, taking initiative, doing ally work, and studying and acting against both the external and internalized forms of oppression and privilege.

Source: "Some Notes for Facilitators" Copyright 2010, by Peggy McIntosh.

Step-by-Step Instructions

Peggy McIntosh wrote "White Privilege" as an autobiographical essay, not a universal essay to speak for all white people everywhere. Use the following protocol to respond to McIntosh's essay.

1. Read McIntosh's essay, "White Privilege" (see end of strategy).

2. Write a reflection on your initial response.

3. Pair-share the reflection.

4. Jot down some of your own experiences with unearned and earned advantages.

5. Write a reflection on these experiences. Describe the situation/s. How did you feel? What did you learn?

6. Pair-share your reflection.

7. Whole-class discussion: Discuss your experiences with this strategy, facilitated by the instructor.

8. Place your written reflections in your professional portfolio.

Looking Back/Looking Ahead

Write about your experience with this strategy—the process and discussions. How might you approach these issues in your own classroom ecosystem?

_____

_____

_____

_____

_____

Content-Area Extensions

Language Arts/History: This strategy provides another lens for viewing multicultural literature and history texts. Students might examine literature anthologies past and present, noticing instances of privilege, i.e., who is foregrounded in the anthology, who receives the most attention in their textbooks. Examine race, class, and gender in these terms.

ADDITIONAL APPLICATION

This strategy serves the same purpose with any group of teachers. It gives both new and veteran teachers a chance to examine privilege and racism in light of their own classrooms and teaching. While there may be some resistance to this strategy, laying the foundation for difficult discussions must begin somewhere, and this particular strategy provides a solid beginning.

WHITE PRIVILEGE: UNPACKING THE INVISIBLE KNAPSACK

By Peggy McIntosh

Through work to bring materials from Women's Studies into the rest of the curriculum, I have often noticed men's unwillingness to grant that they are over-privileged, even though they may grant that women are disadvantaged. They may say they will work to improve women's status, in the society, the university, or the curriculum, but they can't or won't support the idea of lessening men's. Denials which amount to taboos surround the subject of advantages which men gain from women's disadvantages. These denials protect male privilege from being fully acknowledged, lessened, or ended.

Thinking through unacknowledged male privilege as a phenomenon, I realized that since hierarchies in our society are interlocking, there was most likely a phenomenon of white privilege which was similarly denied and protected. As a white person, I realized I had been taught about racism as something which puts others at a disadvantage, but had been taught not to see one of its corollary aspects, white privilege, which puts me at an advantage.

I think whites are carefully taught not to recognize white privilege, as males are taught not to recognize male privilege. So I have begun in an untutored way to ask what it is like to have white privilege. I have come to see white privilege as an invisible package of unearned assets which I can count on cashing in each day, but about which I was "meant" to remain oblivious. White privilege is like an invisible weightless knapsack of special provision, maps, passports, codebooks, visas, clothes, tools, and blank checks.

Describing white privilege makes one newly accountable. As we in Women's Studies work to reveal male privilege and ask men to give up some of their power, so one who writes about having white privilege must ask, "Having described it, what will I do to lessen or end it?" After I realized the extent to which men work from a base of unacknowledged privilege, I understood that much of their oppressiveness was unconscious. Then I remembered the frequent charges from women of color that white women whom they encounter are oppressive. I began to understand why we are justly seen as oppressive, even when we don't see ourselves that way. I began to count the ways in which I enjoy unearned skin privilege and have been conditioned into oblivion about its existence.

My schooling gave me no training in seeing myself as an oppressor, as an unfairly advantaged person, or as a participant in a damaged culture. I was taught to see myself as an individual whose moral state depended on her individual moral will. My schooling followed the pattern my colleague Elizabeth Minnich has pointed out: whites are taught to think of their lives as morally neutral, normative, and average, and also ideal, so that when we work to benefit others, this is seen as work which will allow "them" to be more like "us."

I decided to try to work on myself at least by identifying some of the daily effects of white privilege in my life. I have chosen those conditions which I think in my case *attach somewhat more to skin-color privilege* than to class, religion, ethnic status, or geographical location, though of course all these other factors are intricately intertwined. As far as I can see, my African American co-workers, friends, and acquaintances with whom I come into daily or frequent contact in this particular time, place, and line of work cannot count on most of these conditions.

1. I can if I wish arrange to be in the company of people of my race most of the time.

2. If I should need to move, I can be pretty sure of renting or purchasing housing in an area which I can afford and in which I would want to live.

3. I can be pretty sure that my neighbors in such a location will be neutral or pleasant to me.

4. I can go shopping alone most of the time, pretty well assured that I will not be followed or harassed.

5. I can turn on the television or open to the front page of the paper and see people of my race widely represented.

6. When I am told about our national heritage or about "civilization," I am shown that people of my color made it what it is.

7. I can be sure that my children will be given curricular materials that testify to the existence of their race.

8. If I want to, I can be pretty sure of finding a publisher for this piece on white privilege.

9. I can go into a music shop and count on finding the music of my race represented, into a supermarket and find the staple foods which fit with my cultural traditions, into a hairdresser's shop and find someone who can cut my hair.

10. Whether I use checks, credit cards, or cash, I can count on my skin color not to work against the appearance of financial reliability.

11. I can arrange to protect my children most of the time from people who might not like them.

12. I can swear, or dress in secondhand clothes, or not answer letters, without having people attribute these choices to the bad morals, the poverty, or the illiteracy of my race.

13. I can speak in public to a powerful male group without putting my race on trial.

14. I can do well in a challenging situation without being called a credit to my race.

15. I am never asked to speak for all the people of my racial group.

16. I can remain oblivious of the language and customs of persons of color who constitute the world's majority without feeling in my culture any penalty for such oblivion.

17. I can criticize our government and talk about how much I fear its policies and behavior without being seen as a cultural outsider.

18. I can be pretty sure that if I ask to talk to "the person in charge," I will be facing a person of my race.

19. If a traffic cop pulls me over or if the IRS audits my tax return, I can be sure I haven't been singled out because of my race.

20. I can easily buy posters, postcards, picture books, greeting cards, dolls, toys, and children's magazines featuring people of my race.

21. I can go home from most meetings of organizations I belong to feeling somewhat tied in, rather than isolated, out-of-place, outnumbered, unheard, held at a distance, or feared.

22. I can take a job with an affirmative action employer without having coworkers on the job suspect that I got it because of my race.

23. I can choose public accommodation without fearing that people of my race cannot get in or will be mistreated in the places I have chosen.

24. I can be sure that if I need legal or medical help, my race will not work against me.

25. If my day, week, or year is going badly, I need not ask of each negative episode or situation whether it has racial overtones.

26. I can choose blemish cover or bandages in "flesh" color and have them more or less match my skin.

I repeatedly forgot each of the realizations on this list until I wrote it down. For me white privilege has turned out to be an elusive and fugitive subject. The pressure to avoid it is great, for in facing it I must give up the myth of meritocracy. If these things are true, this is not such a free country; one's life is not what one makes it; many doors open for certain people through no virtues of their own.

In unpacking this invisible knapsack of white privilege, I have listed conditions of daily experience which I once took for granted. Nor did I think of any of the perquisites as bad for the holder. I now think that we need a more finely differentiated taxonomy of privilege, for some of these varieties are only what one would want for everyone in a society, and others give license to be ignorant, oblivious, arrogant, and destructive.

I see a pattern running through the matrix of white privilege, a pattern of assumptions which were passed on to me as a white person. There was one main piece of cultural turf; it was my own turf, and I was among those who could control the turf. *My skin color was an asset for any move I was educated to want to make.* I could think of myself as belonging in major ways, and of making social systems work for me. I could freely disparage, fear, neglect, or be oblivious to anything outside of the dominant cultural forms. Being of the main culture, I could also criticize it fairly freely.

In proportion as my racial group was being made confident, comfortable, and oblivious, other groups were likely being made unconfident, uncomfortable, and alienated. Whiteness protected me from many kinds of hostility, distress, and violence, which I was being subtly trained to visit in turn upon people of color.

For this reason, the word "privilege" now seems to me misleading. We usually think of privilege as being a favored state, whether earned or conferred by birth or luck. Yet some of the conditions I have described here work to systematically overempower certain groups. Such privilege simply *confers dominance* because of one's race or sex.

I want, then, to distinguish between earned strength and unearned power conferred systemically. Power from unearned privilege can look like strength when it is in fact permission to escape or to dominate. But not all of the privileges on my list are inevitably damaging. Some, like the expectation that neighbors will be decent to you, or that your race will not count against you in court, should be the norm in a just society. Others, like the privilege to ignore less powerful people, distort the humanity of the holder as well as the ignored groups.

We might at least start by distinguishing between positive advantages which we can work to spread, and negative types of advantages which unless rejected will always reinforce our present hierarchies. For example, the feeling that one belongs within the human circle, as Native Americans say, should not be seen as privilege for a few. Ideally it is an *unearned entitlement.* At present, since only a few have it, it is an *unearned advantage* for them. This paper results from a process of coming to see that some of the power which I originally saw as attendant on being a human being in the U.S. consisted in *unearned advantage* and *conferred dominance.*

I have met very few men who are truly distressed about systemic, unearned male advantage and conferred dominance. And so one question for me and others like me is whether we will be like them, or whether we will get truly distressed, even outraged, about unearned race advantage and conferred dominance and if so, what we will do to lessen them. In any case, we need to do more work in identifying how they actually affect our daily lives. Many, perhaps most, of our white students in the U.S. think that racism doesn't affect them because they are not people of color; they do not see "whiteness" as a racial identity. In addition, since race and sex are not the only advantaging systems at work, we need similarly to examine the daily experience of having age advantage, or ethnic advantage, or physical ability, or advantage related to nationality, religion, or sexual orientation.

Difficulties and dangers surrounding the task of finding parallels are many. Since racism, sexism, and heterosexism are not the same, the advantaging associated with them should not be seen as the same. In addition, it is hard to disentangle aspects of unearned advantage which rest more on social class, economic class, race, religion, sex, and ethnic identity than on other factors. Still, all of the oppressions are interlocking, as the Combahee River Collective Statement of 1977 continues to remind us eloquently.

One factor seems clear about all the interlocking oppressions. They take both active forms which we can see and embedded forms which as a member of the dominant group one is taught not to see. In my class and place, I did not see myself as a racist because I was taught to recognize racism only in individual acts of meanness by members of my group, never in invisible systems conferring unsought racial dominance on my group from birth.

Disapproving of the systems won't be enough to change them. I was taught to think that racism could end if white individuals changed their attitudes. [But] a "white" skin in the United States opens many doors for the whites whether or not we approve of the way dominance had been conferred on us.

Individual acts can palliate, but cannot end, these problems.

To redesign social systems we need first to acknowledge their colossal unseen dimensions. The silences and denials surrounding privilege are the key political tool here. They keep the thinking about equality or equity incomplete, protecting unearned advantage and conferred dominance by making these taboo subjects. Most talk by whites about equal opportunity seem to me now to be about equal opportunity to try to get into a position of dominance while denying that *systems* of dominance exist.

It seems to me that obliviousness about white advantage, like obliviousness about male advantage, is kept strongly enculturated in the United States so as to maintain the myth of meritocracy, the myth that

democratic choice is equally available to all. Keeping most people unaware that freedom of confident action is there for just a small number of people props up those in power, and serves to keep power in the hands of the same groups that have most of it already.

Though systemic change takes many decades there are pressing questions for me and I imagine for some others like me if we raise our daily consciousness on the perquisites of being light-skinned. What will we do with such knowledge? As we know from watching men, it is an open question whether we will choose to use unearned advantage to weaken hidden systems of advantage and whether we will use any of arbitrarily-awarded power to try to reconstruct power systems on a broader base.

SOMETHING ABOUT THE SUBJECT MAKES IT HARD TO NAME

By Gloria Yamato

Racism—simple enough in structure, yet difficult to eliminate. Racism—pervasive in the U.S. culture to the point that it deeply affects all the local town folk and spills over, negatively influencing the fortunes of folk around the world. Racism is pervasive to the point that we take many of its manifestations for granted, believing "that's life." Many believe that racism can be dealt with effectively in one hellifying workshop, or one hour-long heated discussion. Many actually believe this monster, racism, that has had at least a few hundred years to take root, grow, invade our space and develop subtle variations . . . this mind-funk that distorts thought and action, can be merely wished away. I've run into folks who really think that we can beat this devil, kick this habit, be healed of this disease in a snap. In a sincere blink of a well-intentioned eye, presto-poof racism disappears. "I've dealt with my racism . . . (envision a laying on of hands) . . . Hallelujah! Now I can go to the beach. Well, fine. Go to the beach. In fact, why don't we all go to the beach and continue to work on the sucker over there? Cuz you can't even shave a little piece off this thing called racism in a day, or a weekend, or a workshop.

When I speak of *oppression,* I'm talking about the systematic, institutionalized mistreatment of one

group of people by another for whatever reason. The oppressors are purported to have an innate ability to access economic resources, information, respect, etc., while the oppressed are believed to have a corresponding negative innate ability. The flip side of oppression is *internalized oppression.* Members of the target group are emotionally, physically, and spiritually battered to the point that they begin to actually believe that their oppression is deserved, is their lot in life, is natural and right, and that it doesn't even exist. The oppression begins to feel comfortable, familiar enough that when mean ol' Massa lay down de whip, we got's to pick it up and whack ourselves and each other. Like a virus, it's hard to beat racism, because by the time you come up with a cure, it's mutated to a "new cure-resistant" form. One shot just won't get it. Racism must be attacked from many angles.

The forms of racism that I pick up on these days are 1) aware/blatant racism, 2) aware/covert racism, 3) unaware/unintentional racism, and 4) unaware/self-righteous racism. I can't say that I prefer any one form of racism over the others, because they all look like an itch needing a scratch. I've heard it said (and understandably so) that the aware/blatant form of racism is preferable if one must suffer it. Outright racists will, without apology or confusion, tell us that because of our color we don't appeal to them. If we so choose, we can attempt to get the hell out of their way before we get the sweat knocked out of us. Growing up, aware/covert racism is what I heard many of my elders bemoaning "up north," after having escaped the overt racism "down south." Apartments were suddenly no longer vacant or rents were outrageously high, when black, brown, red, or yellow persons went to inquire about them. Job vacancies were suddenly filled, or we were fired for very vague reasons. It still happens, though the perpetrators really take care to cover their tracks these days. They don't want to get gummed to death or slobbered on by the toothless laws that supposedly protect us from such inequities.

Unaware/unintentional racism drives usually tranquil white liberals wild when they get called on it, and confirms the suspicions of many people of color who feel that white folks are just plain crazy. It has led white people to believe that it's just fine to ask if they can touch my hair (while reaching). They then exclaim over how soft it is, how it does not scratch their hand. It has led whites to assume that bending over backwards and speaking to me in high-pitched (terrified), condescending tones would make up for all the racist wrongs that distort our lives. This type of racism has led whites right to my doorstep, talking 'bout, "We're sorry/we love you and want to make things right," which is fine, and further, "We're gonna give you the opportunity to fix it while we sleep. Just tell us what you need. 'Bye!!"—which ain't fine. With the best of intentions, the best of educations, and the greatest generosity of heart, whites, operating on the misinformation fed to them from day one, will behave in ways that are racist, will perpetuate racism by being "nice" the way we're taught to be nice. You can just "nice" somebody to death with naivete and lack of awareness of privilege. Then there's guilt and the desire to end racism and how the two get all tangled up to the point that people, morbidly fascinated with their guilt, are immobilized. Rather than deal with ending racism, they sit and ponder their guilt and hope nobody notices how awful they are. Meanwhile, racism picks up momentum and keeps on keepin' on.

Now, the newest form of racism that I'm hip to is unaware/self-righteous racism. The "good white" racist attempts to shame Blacks into being blacker, scorns Japanese-Americans who don't speak Japanese, and knows more about the Chicano/a community than the folks who make up the community. They assign themselves as the "good whites," as opposed to the "bad whites," and are often so busy telling people of color what the issues in the Black, Asian, Indian, Latino/a communities should be that they don't have time to deal with their errant sisters and brothers in the white community. Which means that people of color are still left to deal with what the "good whites" don't want to . . . racism.

Internalized racism is what really gets in my way as a Black woman. It influences the way I see or don't see myself, limits what I expect of myself or others like me. It results in my acceptance of mistreatment, leads me to believe that being treated with less than absolute respect, at least this once, is to be expected because I am Black, because I am not white. "Because I am (*you fill in the color*), you think, "Life is going to be hard." The fact is life may be hard, but the color of your skin is not the cause of the hardship. The color of your skin may be used as an excuse to mistreat you, but there is no reason or logic involved in the mistreatment. If it seems that your color is the reason, if it seems that your ethnic heritage is the cause of the woe, it's because you've been deliberately beaten down by agents of a greedy system until you swallowed the garbage. That is the internalization of racism.

Racism is the systematic, institutionalized mistreatment of one group of people by another based on racial heritage. Like every other oppression, racism can be internalized. People of color come to believe misinformation about their particular ethnic group and thus believe that their mistreatment is justified. With that basic vocabulary, let's take a look at how the whole thing works together. Meet "the Ism Family," racism, classism, ageism, adultism, elitism, sexism, heterosexism, physicalism, etc. All these ism's are systematic, that is, not only are these parasites feeding off our lives, they are also dependent on one another for foundation. Racism is supported and reinforced by classism, which is given a foothold and a boost by adultism, which also feeds sexism, which is validated by heterosexism, and so it goes on. You cannot have the "ism" functioning without first effectively installing its flip-side, the internalized version of the ism. Like twins, as one particular form of the ism grows in potency, there is a corresponding increase in its internalized form within the population. Before oppression becomes a specific ism like racism, usually all hell breaks loose. War. People fight attempts to enslave them, or to subvert their will, or to take what they consider theirs, whether that is territory or dignity. It's true that the various elements of racism, while repugnant, would not be able to do very much damage, but for one generally overlooked key piece: power/privilege.

While in one sense we all have power we have to look at the fact that, in our society, people are stratified into various classes and some of these classes have more privilege than others. The owning class has enough power and privilege to not have to give a good whinney what the rest of the folks have on their minds. The power and privilege of the owning class provides the ability to pay off enough of the working class and offer that paid-off group, the middle class, just enough privilege to make it agreeable to do various and sundry oppressive things to other working-class and outright disenfranchised folk, keeping the lid on explosive inequities, at least for a minute. If you're at the bottom of this heap, and you believe the line that says you're there because that's all you're worth, it is at least some small solace to believe that there are others more worthless than you, because of their gender, race, sexual preference . . . whatever. The specific form of power that runs the show here is the power to intimidate. The power to take away the most lives the quickest, and back it up with legal and "divine" sanction, is the very bottom line. It makes the difference between who's holding the racism end of the stick and who's getting beat with it (or beating others as vulnerable as they are) on the internalized racism end of the stick. What I am saying is, while people of color are welcome to tear up their own neighborhoods and each other, everybody knows that you cannot do that to white folks without hell to pay. People of color can be prejudiced against one another and whites, but do not have an ice-cube's chance in hell of passing laws that will get whites sent to relocation camps "for their own protection and the security of the nation." People who have not thought about or refuse to acknowledge this imbalance of power/privilege often want to talk about the racism of people of color. But then that is one of the ways racism is able to continue to function. You look for someone to blame and you blame the victim, who will nine times out often accept the blame out of habit.

So, what can we do? Acknowledge racism for a start, even though and especially when we've struggled to be kind and fair, or struggled to rise above it all. It is hard to acknowledge the fact that racism circumscribes and pervades our lives. Racism must be dealt with on two levels, personal and societal, emotional and institutional. It is possible—and most effective—to do both at the same time. We must reclaim whatever delight we have lost in our own ethnic heritage or heritages. This so-called melting pot has only succeeded in turning us into fast-food gobbling "generics" (as in generic "white folks" who were once Irish, Polish, Russian, English, etc. and "black folks," who were once Ashanti, Bambara, Baule, Yoruba, etc.). Find or create safe places to actually feel what we've been forced to repress each time we were a victim of, witness to or perpetrator of racism, so that we do not continue, like puppets, to act out the past in the present and future. Challenge oppression. Take a stand against it. When you are aware of something oppressive going down, stop the show. At least call it. We become so numbed to racism that we don't even think twice about it, unless it is immediately life-threatening.

Whites who want to be allies to people of color: You can educate yourselves via research and observation rather than rigidly, arrogantly relying solely on interrogating people of color. Do not expect that people of color should teach you how to behave non-oppressively. Do not give into the pull to be lazy. Think, hard. Do not blame people of color for your frustration about racism, but do appreciate the fact that people of color will often help you get in touch with that frustration. Assume that your effort to be a good friend is appreciated, but don't expect or accept gratitude from people of color. Work on racism for your sake, not "their" sake. Assume that you are needed and capable of being a good ally. Know that you'll make mistakes and commit yourself to correcting them and continuing on as an ally, no matter what. Don't give up.

People of color, working through internalized racism: Remember always that you and others like you are completely worthy of respect, completely capable of achieving whatever you take a notion to do. Remember that the term "people of color" refers to a variety of ethnic and cultural backgrounds. These various groups have been oppressed in a variety of ways. Educate yourself about the ways different peoples have been oppressed and how they've resisted that oppression. Expect and insist that whites are capable of being good allies against racism. Don't give up. Resist the pull to give out the "people of color seal of approval" to aspiring white allies. A moment of appreciation is fine, but more than that tends to be less than helpful. Celebrate yourself. Celebrate yourself. Celebrate the inevitable end of racism.

Source: Used with permission of Gloria Yamato.

Gendered Language

Unpacking Common Parlance

Strategy
19

Although gender-neutral language has been standard academic practice since the 1980s, gendered language remains the norm in popular culture and daily experience for most students. As a result, you may find it unnatural and, therefore, difficult to use the neutral terms required in both speech and writing.

This strategy explains why gender-neutral language is so difficult to acquire, and explores the cultural values, attitudes, and beliefs that shape language use. It will help you think about the ways in which your language reflects your mind-set and the importance of saying what you really mean, even if that is more difficult than saying what comes to mind first.

Note: This strategy can also be used to consider the roots of racist language by changing gender-related words to race-related ones in the following section. That there are few if any synonyms for "white" is revealing in itself, a function of power relationships. That is, the dominant race names the minority; it has no need of naming itself.

STEP-BY-STEP INSTRUCTIONS

1. Meet with a group of your classmates. (The group can be as small as 3 or as large as 10.)

2. On a blackboard, whiteboard, transparency, or poster paper, list all the words you can think of that mean "female." Then make a separate list of all the words you can think of that mean "male." These lists will include neutral synonyms, like "girl" and "boy," as well as less neutral terms, like "slut" and "stud." (While this discussion will lead to some language generally considered inappropriate in a classroom, it is not inappropriate for this strategy. The fact that there are many more inappropriate terms for women than there are for men is part of the learning.)

3. Post both lists where everyone can see them. What do you notice?

4. What are the cultural values, attitudes, and beliefs that resulted in this vocabulary? In other words, why is the list for females longer than the list for males? Why is the language for females more demeaning? Why are women linguistically punished for the same behavior for which men are praised? Why are there more diminutives for women than there are for men?

5. Consider the effect this has on the socialization of school-age boys and girls. What needs to happen to socialize children with greater equity? (In some classes, issues discussed in the Additional Application section below may arise as well.)

LOOKING BACK/LOOKING AHEAD

What was it like to do this strategy? How might you use "Gendered Language: Unpacking Common Parlance" in your own classroom?

_____

_____

_____

_____

_____

CONTENT-AREA EXTENSIONS

Because the relationship between language and culture is relevant in almost all the humanities, this strategy can be used in all those subjects with only small changes.

ADDITIONAL APPLICATION

This strategy works similarly for new and veteran teachers. In our experience, however, the older the group, the more negative the reaction, particularly from men. Words like "honey," "sweetie," "doll," and "baby" as synonyms for "woman" are more likely to be seen as terms of endearment rather than diminishments. Many men say these are names they use for their wives or girlfriends, with no negative connotation at all. This can lead to important consideration of the difference between language used in a private setting between intimates, and language used in a public setting between strangers. It also helps explain why men are often surprised—even angered—when women react negatively to what men consider positive. Further, it raises the question of why women can use similar terms for their male partners without prompting a negative reaction.

Code Switching

Language, Dress, and Behavior

Strategy
20

The code-switching activities in this strategy serve to further illuminate the importance of understanding the signs, language, and rules of respect and transaction that are explicit and implicit in the various cultures and contexts that you navigate personally and professionally on a daily basis. Many of you may be familiar with the term code switching from your linguistic courses. For the activities in this section, we will use the following definition: *Code switching* is knowing and using the appropriate language, behavior, or dress in particular contexts or cultures.

The following strategy illustrates how the choices you make regarding language, behavior, and clothing impact your own life and will impact your future classroom. In your own classrooms and school buildings, you will want to make the guidelines for interaction transparent so that all students can navigate the classroom and school system successfully.

NOTE TO INSTRUCTOR

These code-switching activities provide the perfect opportunity to discuss the importance of developing a professional self who understands the need for professional parlance, behavior, and dress. Moving from inductive to deductive thinking gives students the opportunity to make their own meaning and internalize that meaning regarding language, behavior, and attire.

We further suggest that you extend students' thinking beyond themselves to provide a deeper understanding of code switching in the multicultural universe in which they live. In this light, you might have students read and discuss "How to Tame a Wild Tongue," by Gloria Anzaldúa (1999), which is included at the end of this strategy. For Anzaldúa's essay, you may follow any one of the discussion protocols found in this section or Section IV, and also ask students to make connections between her essay, their observations, and future classrooms.

Step-by-Step Instructions

1. Divide your notebook page into four columns or quarters. Write the following headings for each column: Column I: Language; Column 2: Behavior; Column 3: Clothing/Dress; Column 4: Choices & Consequences.

2. Column I: Language—Brainstorm and list the various ways in which you use language with different audiences and in different cultures and contexts.

   For example, when writing an e-mail to a professor, you write in a more formal tone and style. But when writing to your siblings or a friend, you might use abbreviations and text-message slang. Your tone and style might change if you wanted to borrow money from a family member, friend, or bank loan officer. The banking example also illustrates how behavior might change from context to context. If applying for a loan from your bank, you would fill out forms, make appointments, and meet with a bank officer. If you asked your brother Joe for a loan, you would likely just stop by his house.

3. Column 2: Behavior—Brainstorm the various ways in which you change behaviors with different audiences and in different cultures and contexts. List these in Column 2. As noted in the banking example, some situations are more formal than others and require different types of behavior, e.g., making appointments versus dropping by a friend's apartment.

4. Column 3: Clothing/Dress—Brainstorm and list the various ways in which you change your attire when navigating social ecosystems.

   For example, when at home, Mary wears sweat pants and t-shirts, but at work she wears a suit. Attending a small eastern liberal arts college, Andrea was required to wear skirts to meals and only wore slacks to the cafeteria on weekends. In contrast, Mary attended a large university in the Southwest where blue jeans and t-shirts were the norm. Our choices of clothing and dress depend on different cultures, contexts, and time periods.

5. Column 4: Choices & Consequences—Why do you shift from one language/behavior/dress in any given situation? What might be the consequences for not code switching from one venue to the next? Why? Should we need to code switch? Why or why not?

6. Whole-class discussion: Use column topics as discussion starters.

7. Place this material in your professional portfolio.

Looking Back/Looking Ahead

Write about your experience with this strategy. How is this strategy related to your emerging and future professional self? How might you use the "Code Switching" strategy in your future classroom?

_____

_____

_____

_____

_____

CONTENT-AREA EXTENSIONS

Language Arts/Social Studies: When reading literature, students can examine characters in light of code switching and choices and consequences. Do characters code switch when interacting with other characters. Why? What choices does the character make? What are the consequences?

History: Students can examine the choices and consequences made by historical figures.

Communication: Students can examine multicultural situations through the lens of code switching.

ADDITIONAL APPLICATION

New and veteran teachers can do this strategy with their own classrooms in mind. What types of language, behavior, and dress are appropriate in their classroom, building, or school system? Making connections between this strategy and Strategy 12, "Shared Language and Guidelines," as well as Strategy 22, "Campus Culture Walk," can be especially powerful when teachers examine their own classrooms, buildings, and school systems and the explicit and implicit consequences of the guidelines and rules of interaction.

HOW TO TAME A WILD TONGUE

By Gloria Anzaldúa

"We're going to have to control your tongue," the dentist says, pulling out all the metal from my mouth. Silver bits plop and tinkle into the basin. My mouth is a motherlode.

The dentist is cleaning out my roots. I get a whiff of the stench when I gasp. "I can't cap that tooth yet, you're still draining," he says.

"We're going to have to do something about your tongue," I hear the anger rising in his voice. My tongue keeps pushing out the wads of cotton, pushing back the drills, the long thin needles. "I've never seen anything as strong or as stubborn," he says. And I think, how do you tame a wild tongue, train it to be quiet, how do you bridle and saddle it? How do you make it lie down?

> Who is to say that robbing a people of its language is less violent than war?
>
> —Ray Gwyn Smith[1]

I remember being caught speaking Spanish at recess—that was good for three licks on the knuckles with a sharp ruler. I remember being sent to the corner of the classroom for "talking back" to the Anglo teacher when all I was trying to do was tell her how to pronounce my name. "If you want to be American, speak 'American.' If you don't like it, go back to Mexico where you belong."

"I want you to speak English. *Pa' hallar buen trabajo tienes que saber habloar el ingles bien. Qué vale toda tu educación si todavía hablas ingles con un 'accent,'*" my mother would say, mortified that I spoke English like a Mexican. At Pan American University, I and all Chicano students were required to take two speech classes. Their purpose: to get rid of our accents.

Attacks on one's form of expression with the intent to censor are a violation of the First Amendment. *El Anglo con cara de inocente nos arrancó la lengua.* Wild tongues can't be tamed, they can only be cut out.

OVERCOMING THE TRADITION OF SILENCE

Ahogadas, escupimos el oscuro.
Peleando con nuestra propia sombra
El silencio nos sepulta.

En boca cerrada no entran moscas

"Flies don't enter a closed mouth" is a saying I kept hearing when I was a child. *Ser habladora* was to be a gossip and a liar, to talk too much. *Muchachitas bien criadas,* well-bred girls don't answer back. *Es una falta de respeto* to talk back to one's mother or father. I remember one of the sins I'd recite to the priest in the confession box the few times I went to confession: talking back to my mother, *hablor pa' 'tras, repelar. Hociocona, repelona, chismosa,* having a big mouth, questioning, carrying tales are all signs of being *mal criada.* In my culture they are all words that are derogatory if applied to women—I've never heard them applied to men.

The first time I heard two women, a Puerto Rican and a Cuban, say the word *"nosotras"* I was shocked. I had not known the word existed. Chicanas use *nosotros* [we] whether we're male or female. We are robbed of our female being by the masculine plural. Language is a male discourse.

> And our tongues have become dry, the
> wilderness has dried out our tongues and
> we have forgotten speech.
>
> —Irena Klepfisz[2]

Even our own people, other Spanish speakers *nos quieren poner candados en la boca.* They would hold us back with their bag of *reglas de academia.*

> Oyé como ladra el lenguaje de la frontera
> Quien tiene boca se equivoca.
>
> —Mexican saying

"*Pocho,* cultural traitor, you're speaking the oppressor's language by speaking English, you're ruining the Spanish language," I have been accused by various Latinos and Latinas. Chicano Spanish is considered by the purist and by most Latinos deficient, a mutilation of Spanish.

But Chicano Spanish is a border tongue which developed naturally. Change, *evolución, enriquecimiento de palabras nuevas por invención .o adopción* have created variants of Chicano Spanish, *un Nuevo lenguaje. Un lenguaje que corresponde a un modo de vivir.* Chicano Spanish is not incorrect, it is a living language.

For a people who are neither Spanish nor live in a country in which Spanish is the first language; for a people who live in a country in which English is the reigning tongue but who are not Anglo; for a people who cannot entirely identify with either standard (formal, Castilian) Spanish nor standard English, what recourse is left to them but to create their own language? A language which they can connect their identity to, one capable of communicating the realities and values true to themselves—a language with terms that are neither *español ni ingles,* but both. We speak a patois, a forked tongue, a variation of two languages.

Chicano Spanish sprang out of the Chicanos' need to identify ourselves as a distinct people. We needed a language with which we could communicate with ourselves, a secret language. For some of us, language is a homeland closer than the Southwest—for many Chicanos today live in the Midwest and the East. And because we are a complex, heterogeneous people, we speak many languages. Some of the languages we speak are

1. Standard English

2. Working-class and slang English

3. Standard Spanish

4. Standard Mexican Spanish

5. North Mexican Spanish

6. Chicano Spanish (Texas, New Mexico, Arizona, and California have regional variations)

7. Tex-Mex

8. *Pachuco (called caló)*

My "home" tongues are the languages I speak with my sister and brothers, with my friends. They are the last five listed, with 6 and 7 being closest to my heart. From school, the media, and job situations, I've picked up standard and working-class English. From Mamagrande Locha and from reading Spanish and Mexican literature, I've picked up Standard Spanish and Standard Mexican Spanish. From *los recién llegados,* Mexican immigrants, and *braceros,* I learned the North Mexican dialect. With Mexicans I'll try to speak either Standard Mexican Spanish or the North Mexican dialect. From my parents and Chicanos living in the valley, I picked up Chicano Texas Spanish, and I speak it with my mom, younger brother (who married a Mexican and who rarely mixes Spanish with English), aunts, and older relatives.

With Chicanas from *Nuevo México* or *Arizona* I will speak Chicano Spanish a little, but often they don't understand what I'm saying. With most California Chicanas I speak entirely in English (unless I forget). When I first moved to San Francisco, I'd rattle off something in Spanish, unintentionally embarrassing them. Often it is only with another Chicana *tejano* that I can talk freely.

Words distorted by English are known as anglicisms or *pochismos*. The *pocho* is an anglicized Mexican or American of Mexican origin who speaks Spanish with an accent characteristic of North Americans and who distorts and reconstructs the language according to the influence of English.[3] Tex-Mex, or Spanglish, comes most naturally to me. I may switch back and forth from English to Spanish in the same sentence or in the same word. With my sister and my brother Nune and with Chicano *tejano* contemporaries I speak in Tex-Mex.

From kids and people my own age I picked up *Pachuco. Pachuco* (the language of the zoot suiters) is a language of rebellion, both against Standard Spanish and Standard English. It is a secret language. Adults of the culture and outsiders cannot understand it. It is made up of slang words from both English and Spanish. *Ruca* means girl or woman, *vato* means guy or dude, *chale* means no, *simón* means yes, *churro* is sure, talk is *periquiar*, *pigionear* means petting, *que gacho* means how nerdy, *ponte águila* means watch out, death is called *la perlona*. Through lack of practice and not having others who can speak it, I've lost most of the *Pachuco* tongue.

CHICANO SPANISH

Chicanos, after 250 years of Spanish/Anglo colonization, have developed significant differences in the Spanish we speak. We collapse two adjacent vowels into a single syllable and sometimes shift the stress in certain words such as *maíz/maiz*, *cohete/cuete.* We leave out certain consonants when they appear between vowels: *lado/lao*, *mojado/mojao.* Chicanos from South Texas pronounce *f* as *j* as in *jue (fue).* Chicanos use "archaisms," words that are no longer in the Spanish language, words that have been evolved out. We say *semos, truje, haiga, ansina,* and *naiden.* We retain the "archaic" *j*, as in *jalar*, that derives from an earlier *h* (the French *halar* or the Germanic *halon* which was lost to standard Spanish in the sixteenth century), but which is still found in several regional dialects such as the one spoken in South Texas. (Due to geography, Chicanos from the Valley of South Texas were cut off linguistically from other Spanish speakers. We tend to use words that the Spaniards brought over from Medieval Spain. The majority of the Spanish colonizers in Mexico and the Southwest came from Extremadura—Hernán Cortés was one of them—and Andalucía. Andalucians pronounce *ll* like a *y*, and their *d*'s tend to be absorbed by adjacent vowels: *tirade* becomes *tirao.* They brought *el lenguaje popular, dialectos, y regionalismos.*[4]

Chicanos and other Spanish speakers also shift *ll* to *y* and *z* to *s*.[5] We leave out initial syllables, saying *tar* for *estar, toy* for *estoy, hora* for *ahora* (*cubanos* and *puertorriqueños* also leave out initial letters of some words). We also leave out the final syllable such as *pa* for *para.* The intervocalic *y*, the *ll* as in *tortilla, ella, botella,* gets replaced by *tortia* or *toriya, ea, botea.* We add an additional syllable at the beginning of certain words: *atocar* for *tocar, agastar* for *gastar.* Sometimes we'll say *lavaste las vacijas,* other times *lavates* (substituting the *ates* verb endings for the *aste*).

We use anglicisms, words borrowed from English: *bola* from ball, *carpeta* from carpet, *machine de lavar* (instead of *lavadora*) from washing machine. Tex-Mex argot, created by adding a Spanish sound at the beginning or end of an English word such as *cookiar* for cook, *watcher* for watch, *parkiar* fo park, and *rapiar* for rape, is the result of the pressures on Spanish speakers to adapt to English.

We don't use the word *vosotros/as* or its accompanying verb form. We don't say *claro* (to mean yes), *imagínate,* or *me emociona,* unless we picked up Spanish from Latinas, out of a book, or in a classroom. Other Spanish-speaking groups are going through the same, or similar, development in their Spanish.

LINGUISTIC TERRORISM

Deslenguadas. Somos los del español deficient.

We are your linguistic nightmare, your linguistic aberration, your linguistic *mestisaje,* the subject of your *burla.* Because we speak with tongues of fire we are culturally crucified. Racially, culturally, and linguistically *somos huérfanos*—we speak an orphan tongue.

Chicanas who grew up speaking Chicano Spanish have internalized the belief that we speak poor Spanish. It is illegitimate, a bastard language. And because we internalize how our language has been used against us by the dominant culture, we use our language differences against each other.

Chicana feminists often skirt around each other with suspicion and hesitation. For the longest time I couldn't figure it out. Then it dawned on me. To be close to another Chicana is like looking into the mirror. We are afraid of what we'll see there. *Pena.* Shame. Low estimation of self. In childhood we are told that our language is wrong. Repeated attacks on our native tongue diminish our sense of self. The attacks continue throughout our lives.

Chicanas feel uncomfortable talking Spanish to Latinas, afraid of their censure. Their language was not outlawed in their countries. They had a whole lifetime of being immersed in their native tongue; generations, centuries in which Spanish was a first language, taught in school, heard on radio and TV, and read in the newspaper.

If a person, Chicana or Latina, has a low estimation of my native tongue, she also has a low estimation of me. Often with *mexicanas y latinas* we'll speak English as a neutral language. Even among Chicanas we tend to speak English at parties or conferences. Yet, at the same time, we're afraid the other will think we're *agringadas* because we don't speak Chicano Spanish. We oppress each other trying to out-Chicano each other, vying to be the "real" Chicanas, to speak like Chicanos. There is no one Chicano language just as there is no one Chicano experience. A monolingual Chicana whose first language is English or Spanish is just as much a Chicana as one who speaks several variants of Spanish. A Chicana from Michigan or Chicago or Detroit is just as much a Chicana as one from the Southwest. Chicano Spanish is as diverse linguistically as it is regionally.

By the end of this [the twentieth] century, Spanish speakers will comprise the biggest minority group in the United States, a country where students in high schools and colleges are encouraged to take French classes because French is considered more "cultured." But for a language to remain alive it must be used.[6] By the end of this century English, and not Spanish, will be the mother tongue of most Chicanos and Latinos.

So, if you want to really hurt me, talk badly about my language. Ethnic identity is twin skin to linguistic identity—I am my language. Until I can take pride in my language, I cannot take pride in myself. Until I can accept as legitimate Chicano Texas Spanish, Tex-Mex, and all other languages I speak, I cannot accept the legitimacy of myself. Until I am free to write bilingually and to switch codes without having always to translate, while I still have to speak English or Spanish when I would rather speak Spanglish, and as long as I have to accommodate the English speaker rather than having them accommodate me, my tongue will be illegitimate.

I will no longer be made to feel ashamed of existing. I will have my voice: Indian, Spanish, white. I will have my serpent's tongue—my woman's voice, my sexual voice, my poet's voice. I will overcome the tradition of silence.

> *My fingers*
> *Move sly against your palm*
> *Like women everywhere, we speak in code.*
>
> —Melanie Kaye/Kantrowitz[7]

"Vistas," corridos, y comida: My Native Tongue

In the 1960's, I read my first Chicano novel. It was *City of Night* by John Rechy, a gay Texan, son of a Scottish father and a Mexican mother. For days I walked around in stunned amazement that a Chicano could write and could get published. When I read *I Am Joaquín*[8] I was surprised to see a bilingual book by a Chicano in print. When I saw poetry written in Tex-Mex for the first time, a feeling of pure joy flashed through me. I felt like we really existed as a people. In 1971, when I started teaching High School English to Chicano students, I tried to supplement the required texts with works by Chicanos, only to be reprimanded and forbidden to do so by the principal. He claimed that I was supposed to teach

"American" and English literature. At risk of being fired, I swore my students to secrecy and slipped in Chicano short stories, poems, a play. In graduate school, while working toward a Ph.D., I had to "argue" with one advisor after the other, semester after semester, before I was allowed to make Chicano literature an area of focus.

Even before I read books by Chicanos or Mexicans, it was the Mexican movies I saw at the drive-in—the Thursday night special of $1.00 a carload—that gave me a sense of belonging. *"Vámonos a las vistas,"* my mother would call out and we'd all—grandmother, brothers, sister, and cousins—squeeze into the car. We'd wolf down cheese and bologna white bread sandwiches while watching Pedro Infante in melodramatic tearjerkers like *Nosotros los pobres,* the first "real" Mexican movie (that was not an imitation of European movies). I remember seeing *Cuando los hijos se van* and surmising that all Mexican movies played up the love a mother has for her children and what ungrateful sons and daughters suffer when they are not devoted to their mothers. I remember the singing-type "westerns" of Jorge Negrete and Miguel Aceves Mejía. When watching Mexican movies, I felt a sense of homecoming as well as alienation. People who were to amount to something didn't go to Mexican movies, or *bailes,* or tune their radios to *bolero, rancherita,* and *corrido* music.

The whole time I was growing up, there was *norteño* music, sometimes called North Mexican border music, or Tex-Mex music, or Chicano music, or *cantina* (bar) music. I grew up listening to *conjuntos,* three- or four-piece bands made up of folk musicians playing guitar, *bajo sexton,* drums, and button accordion, which Chicanos had borrowed from the German immigrants who had come to Central Texas and Mexico to farm and build breweries. In the Rio Grande Valley, Steven Jordan and Little Joe Hernández were popular, and Flaco Jiménez was the accordion king. The rhythms of Tex-Mex music are those of the polka, also adapted from the Germans, who in turn had borrowed the polka from the Czechs and Bohemians.

I remember the hot, sultry evenings when *corridos*—songs of love and death on the Texas-Mexican borderlands—reverberated out of cheap amplifiers from the local *cantinas* and wafted in through my bedroom window.

Corridos first became widely used along the South Texas/Mexican border during the early conflict between Chicanos and Anglos. The *corridos* are usually about Mexican heroes who do valiant deeds against the Anglo oppressors. Pancho Villa's song, *"La cucaracha,"* is the most famous one. *Corridos* of John F. Kennedy and his death are still very popular in the Valley. Older Chicanos remember Lydia Mendoza, one of the great border *corrido* singers who was called *la Gloris de Tejas.* Her *"El tango negro,"* sung during the Great Depression, made her a singer of the people. The ever-present *corridos* narrated one hundred years of border history, bringing news of events as well as entertaining. These folk musicians and folk songs are our chief cultural mythmakers, and they made our hard lives seem bearable.

I grew up feeling ambivalent about our music. Country-western and rock-and-roll had more status. In the fifties and sixties, for the slightly educated and *agringado* Chicanos, there existed a sense of shame at being caught listening to our music. Yet I couldn't stop feet from thumping to the music, could not stop humming the words, nor hide from myself the exhilaration I felt when I heard it.

There are more subtle ways that we internalize identification, especially in the forms of images and emotions. For me food and certain smells are tied to my identity, to my homeland. Woodsmoke curling up to an immense blue sky; woodsmoke perfuming my grandmother's clothes, her skin. The stench of cow manure and the yellow patches on the ground; the crack of a .22 rifle and the reek of cordite. Homemade white cheese sizzling in a pan, melting inside a folded *tortilla.* My sister Hilda's hot, spicy *menudo, chile Colorado* making it deep red, pieces of *panza* and hominy floating on top. My brother Carito barbequing *fajitas* in the backyard. Even now and 3,000 miles away, I can see my mother spicing the ground beef, pork, and venison with *chile.* My mouth salivates at the thought of the hot steaming *tamales* I would be eating if I were home.

SI LE PREGUNTAS A MI MAMA, "QUÉ ERES?"

Identity is the essential core of who
we are as individuals, the conscious experience of
the self inside.

—Gershen Kaufman[9]

Nosotros los Chicanos straddle the borderlands. On one side of us, we are constantly exposed to the

Spanish of the Mexicans, on the other side we hear the Anglos' incessant clamoring so that we forget our language. Among ourselves we don't say *nosotros los americanos, o nosotros los españoles, o nosotros los hispanos.* We say *nosotros los mexicanos* (by *mexicanos* we do not mean citizens of Mexico; we do not mean a national identity, but a racial one). We distinguish between *mexicanos del otro lado* and *Mexicanos de este lado.* Deep in our hearts we believe that being Mexican has nothing to do with which country one lives in. Being Mexican is a state of soul—not one of mind, not one of citizenship. Neither eagle nor serpent, but both. And like the ocean, neither animal respects borders.

> Dime con quien andas y te dire quien eres.
> *(Tell me who your friends are and I'll tell you who you are.)*
>
> —Mexican saying

Si le preguntas a mi mamá, "¿Qué eres?" te dirá, "Soy Mexicana." My brothers and sister say the same. I sometimes will answer *"soy mexicana"* and at others will say *"soy Chicana" o "soy tejana."* But I identified as *"Raza"* before I ever identified as *"mexicana" or "Chicana."*

As a culture, we call ourselves Spanish when referring to ourselves as a linguistic group and when copping out. It is then that we forget our predominant Indian genes. We are 70–80 percent Indian.[10] We call ourselves Hispanic[11] or Spanish-American or Latin American or Latin when linking ourselves to other Spanish-speaking peoples of the western hemisphere and when copping out. We call ourselves Mexican-American[12] to signify we are neither Mexican nor American, but more the noun "American" than the adjective "Mexican" (and when copping out).

Chicanos and other people of color suffer economically for not acculturating. This voluntary (yet forced) alienation makes for psychological conflict, a kind of dual identity—we don't identify with the Mexican cultural values. We are a synergy of two cultures with various degrees of Mexicanness or Angloness. I have so internalized the borderland conflict that sometimes I feel one cancels out the other and we are zero, nothing, no one. *A veces no soy nada ni nadie. Pero hasta cuando no lo soy, lo soy.*

When not copping out, when we know we are more than nothing, we call ourselves Mexican, referring to race and ancestry; *mestizo* when affirming both our Indian and Spanish (but we hardly ever own our Black) ancestry; Chicano when referring to a politically aware people born and/or raised in the United States; *Raza* when referring to Chicanos; *tejanos* when we are Chicanos from Texas.

Chicanos did not know we were a people until 1965 when Cesar Chavez and the farmworkers united and *I Am Joaquín* was published and *la Raza Unida* party was formed in Texas. With that recognition, we became a distinct people. Something momentous happened to the Chicano soul—we became aware or our reality and acquired a name and a language (Chicano Spanish) that reflected that reality. Now that we had a name, some of the fragmented pieces began to fall together—who we were, what we were, how we had evolved. We began to get glimpses of what we might eventually become.

Yet the struggle of identities continues, the struggle of borders is our reality still. One day the inner struggle will cease and a true integration take place. In the meantime, *tenémos que hacer la lucha. ¿Quién está protegiendo los ranchos de mi gente? ¿Quién está tratando de cerrar la fisura entre la india y el blanco en nuestra sangre? El Chicano gue anda como un ladrón en su propia casa.*

Los Chicanos, how patient we seem, how very patient. There is the quiet of the Indian about us.[13] We know how to survive. When other races have given up their tongue we've kept ours. We know what it is to live under the hammer blow of the dominant *norteamericano* culture. But more than we count the blows, we count the days the weeks the years the centuries the aeons until the white laws and commerce and customs will rot in the deserts they've created, lie bleached. *Humildes* yet proud, *quietos* yet wild, about our business. Stubborn, persevering, impenetrable as stone, yet possessing a malleability that renders us unbreakable, we, the *mestizas* and *mestizos,* will remain.

NOTES

1. Ray Gwyn Smith, *Moorland Is Cold Country,* unpublished book.

2. Irena Klepfisz, "*Di rayxe aheym* / The Journey Home," in *The Tribe of Dina: A Jewish Women's Anthology,* edited by Melanie Kaye/Kantrowitz and Irena Klepfisz (Montpelier, VT: Sinister Wisdom Books, 1986), 49.

3. R. C. Ortega, *Dialectología Del Barrio*, translated by Hortencia S. Alwan (Los Angeles: R. C. Ortega, 1977), 132.

4. Eduardo Hernandéz-Chávez, Andrew D. Cohen, and Anthony F. Beltramo, *El Lenguaje de los Chicanos: Regional and Social Characteristics of Language Used by Mexican Americans* (Arlington, VA: Center for Applied Linguistics, 1975), 39.

5. Hernandéz-Chávez, xvii.

6. Irena Klepfisz, "Secular Jewish Identity: Yidishkayt in America," in *The Tribe of Dina*, edited by Kaye/Kantrowitz and Irena Klepfisz, (Montpelier, VT: Sinister Wisdom Books, 1986), 43.

7. Melanie Kaye/Kantrowitz, "Sign," in *We Speak in Code: Poems and Other Writings* (Pittsburgh: Motheroot Publications, 1980), 85.

8. Rodolfo Gonzales, *I Am Joaquín* (New York: Bantam Books, 1972; first published in 1967).

9. Gershen Kaufman, *Shame: The Power of Caring* (Cambridge, MA: Schenkman Books, 1980), 68.

10. John R. Chávez, *The Lost Land: The Chicano Images of the Southwest* (Albuquerque: University of New Mexico Press, 1984), 88–90.

11. "Hispanic" is derived from *Hispanis (España,* a name given to the Iberian Peninsula in ancient times when it was a part of the Roman Empire) and is a term designated by the U.S. government to make it easier to handle us on paper.

12. The Treaty of Guadalupe Hidalgo created the Mexican-American in 1848.

13. Anglos, in order to alleviate their guilt for dispossessing the Chicano, stressed the Spanish part of us and perpetrated the myth of the Spanish Southwest. We have accepted the fiction that we are Hispanic, that is, Spanish, in order to accommodate ourselves to the dominant culture and its abhorrence of Indians (Chávez, 1984, 88–91; see note 10 above).

Being and Becoming

Bullies and Divas and Martyrs, Oh My!

Strategy
21

RATIONALE

You have come full circle. You began this section thinking about who you are—and who you are not—as you interact with others in the various social ecosystems of your daily life. By the end of the section, your thinking will have moved into the classroom to consider how a person's values, beliefs, language, and behavior impact their own and others' equilibrium and their learning. In this strategy, the focus is explicitly on who you are being and becoming as a member of the classroom culture.

Group work most clearly illustrates this role-playing point. Group work takes many forms—project teams, literature circles, or writing response groups among them. Aside from its established value as a content-learning strategy, group work is an opportunity to learn more about yourself—who you *think* you are and who you actually are being, which may be disturbingly different.

This strategy works best when connected to an actual group-work experience. It requires only that after the assigned group work is done, you think about the role you played and write a brief analysis of (1) who you were in the group; (2) what you contributed to the effort; and (3) how you responded to others, identified by their roles, not their names. These individual analyses can be handed in with the final group project and can be factored into individual grades on the project.

STEP-BY-STEP INSTRUCTIONS

1. Read the excerpt from "Feuds in Student Groups: Coping With Whiners, Martyrs, Saboteurs, Bullies, and Deadbeats" (Jalajas & Sutton, 1984), found at the end of this strategy.

2. Small-group discussion: Which of these characters do you recognize from your own experience in groups? What other roles have you played or have you seen others play? (Additional possibilities include everything from Diva and Drama Queen (or -King) to Freeloader, Ghost, and BFF.)

3. Whole-class discussion: What positive roles are there? Compile a list the whole class can see. Examples might include Mediator, Mentor, Collaborator, Organizer, or Cheerleader.

4. Write a one-page analysis of your recent group experience. Who were you being? What did you contribute to the group effort? How did you respond to any negative behavior of others? (Note: Do not use the names of your partners. Refer to them only categorically, e.g., "We had a bully in our group.")

5. What did you learn from this experience that may inform your group-work experiences in the future? Your use of groups as a teacher?

6. Place your analysis in your professional portfolio.

Looking Back/Looking Ahead

What was it like to do this strategy? How might you use "Being and Becoming: Bullies and Divas and Martyrs, Oh My!" in your own classroom?

_____

_____

_____

_____

_____

Content-Area Extensions

Language Arts: This lens can be used to think about relationships between characters in literature.

Social Studies: This lens can be used to understand historical conflicts between individuals or cultures.

Additional Application

This strategy can be done the same way with new or veteran teachers.

FEUDS IN STUDENT GROUPS: COPING WITH WHINERS, MARTYRS, SABOTEURS, BULLIES, AND DEADBEATS*

Interdependence creates an arena in which students with different perspectives and a common assignment may fight. . . . Students with diverse backgrounds may also feud because of differences in world view and language. Nevertheless, as teachers, we rarely hear about such structural factors from feuding students. Rather we hear complaints about troublesome individuals.

We have noticed that such troublesome characters fall into distinguishable categories. We have identified five "types" of students that are associated with conflict in student groups. We are not attributing fault to these people, but we have observed that conflict tends to be more common in groups that don't manage them well. The characters we have identified are The Whiner, The Martyr, The Saboteur, The Bully, and The Deadbeat.

The Whiner

The group project is one hassle after another for The Whiner. The Whiner feels that the group meets on the most inconvenient day and time, the paper is turning out to be too long, and nobody else is contributing as much to the project. The Whiner can't see how the project will be any good or be done on time. . . . The group may become diverted from the project to mollify The Whiner. Such activity can often lead to an inordinate weighting of The Whiner's input at the expense of more valuable, but less vociferous, contributions by others in the group. Moreover, the unnecessary anxiety of approaching a group meeting containing The Whiner can be unpleasant, lead to fewer meetings than might be necessary, and hamper the effectiveness in meetings that are held.

The Martyr

The Martyr is certain that he or she is getting the worst assignment, the worst chores to perform, and has the dumbest partners for group members. The Martyr may complain to other group members, or to the instructor, about the burden. Yet, in contrast to The Whiner, The Martyr doesn't seem to want anything to change; he or she just wants others to feel guilty. The Martyr tells the other group members, "It's okay. Go skiing, I don't mind doing the paper."

The Saboteur

In contrast to The Martyr and The Whiner, The Saboteur takes an active role in the disruption of the group. Such disruption is often unintentional; the student may only be trying to enhance the quality of the group's work. The Saboteur's trademark is that these "enhancements" are implemented without the knowledge of the other group members. Unfortunately for the group, the altered work may be of lower quality than the original. . . .

The Bully

This character also takes an active role in the disruption of the group, but unlike The Saboteur, The Bully isn't shy about letting the group know how things should be done. The Bully's special talent is making others in the group feel inadequate or dumb. This problem is accentuated if The Bully is either brighter or better prepared than the others in the group. If the superior ability of The Bully is clear to the other members, they may be unwilling to contribute anything to the project. Alternately, a backlash may develop within the group; other members may choose to ignore The Bully or to argue with everything The Bully says.

A variation on "The Bully" is "The Lazy Bully." The Lazy Bully plays no active role in the group until some critical decision must be made. At this juncture, The Lazy Bully tries to force his or her will on the other members of the group. This character is disruptive because coworkers resent The Lazy Bully's newfound interest in the group task. . . .

The Deadbeat

The Whiner, The Martyr, The Saboteur, and The Bully each take actions that disrupt the group. The Deadbeat doesn't necessarily disrupt anything. Yet The Deadbeat can evoke feuds when other group members refuse to carry an unproductive member. Members may decide that "something must be done" about The Deadbeat and spend an inordinate amount of time deciding how to cope with their idle coworker. They may even spend time fighting with The Deadbeat.

*Source: From "Feuds in Student Groups: Coping With Whiners, Martyrs, Saboteurs, Bullies and Deadbeats," by D. Jalajas & R. Sutton, 1984, *Journal of Management Education, 9,* 4.

Campus Culture Walk

Strategy 22

In Section II, you have had the opportunity to examine who you are as you interact with others in various social ecosystems, and you have considered how a person's values, attitudes, and beliefs impact the classroom culture. In this final strategy, you will step outside the intimacy of the classroom to explore the campus ecosystem.

The classroom ecosystem is nested in the larger ecosystem of the school building and campus. School buildings and campuses have personalities of their own, and while each and every classroom may influence the environment outside the classroom door, so in turn do the various groups and administrators on campus influence the culture and climate inside the classroom. This strategy gives you the opportunity to look at your own college campus and its culture to find out what values, attitudes, and beliefs are conveyed through visible artifacts such as posters, statues, building organization, and so on. The purpose of this strategy is for you to begin thinking about the synergistic nature of ecosystems and how they influence each other, and more specifically, the impact that these ecosystems may have on your future classroom ecosystem.

STEP-BY-STEP INSTRUCTIONS

1. Pair up: In this strategy, you and another classmate will select a particular building, outdoor area, or single hallway on your campus to examine as a manifestation of culture. (Use this definition of *culture*: the set of shared attitudes, values, goals, and practices that characterize an institution, organization, or group.)

2. Select an area of campus to study; take your notebooks and begin your culture walk. In your notebook, list any objects, posters, flyers, school mascots, books, or items of interest you notice. Jot down as many details as possible. Look for patterns of values, attitudes, or beliefs in the artifacts. List at least 10 artifacts.

   For example, our students might notice the bronze ram in the middle of campus, the football player calendar displayed in the main hall; pep rally posters; a flyer advertising a lecture on the dynamics of diversity; and the posters advertising the Lesbian, Gay, Bisexual, Transgender (LGBT) Organization meeting.

3. Analysis: Once you feel you have gathered enough information about your school climate and culture, it's time to do a mini analysis of how the different artifacts illustrate your college's culture and climate. Are there patterns in the materials and artifacts that you noted?

   In the list our students compiled above, they found that many artifacts indicated a focus on sports, a climate of school spirit, and an openness to diversity.

4. Analyze at least 4–8 artifacts. Decide what these artifacts, taken together, say about the climate and culture of your campus. How might these artifacts influence the atmosphere of the classroom ecosystem?

5. Whole-class discussion: Discuss commonalities and differences in your observations of the school culture and climate. What did you notice? What did you wonder? What surprised you?

6. Include your notes for this strategy in your professional portfolio.

Looking Back/Looking Ahead

Write about your experience with this strategy—the process, product, and discussions. How might you use the "Campus Culture Walk" in your field experience? In your future classroom?

_____

_____

_____

_____

_____

Content-Area Extensions

Across the Curriculum: This strategy can be translated into a *text walk* in which students examine the table of contents/photographs/graphs to decide what values, attitudes, and beliefs are in the foreground and which are in the background.

Additional Application

This strategy serves the same purpose with any group of teachers. It gives both new and veteran teachers a chance to examine their own schools through fresh eyes.

SECTION III

Introduction to Classroom Inquiry

Like the biological and social scientists who study ecosystems, teachers need to study their classroom ecosystems in order to support and ensure their sustainability. Because populations change, materials change, and environmental conditions change, teacher inquiry is particularly crucial to create and sustain these ecosystems. According to Lisa Delpit (cited in Hubbard & Power, 2003), to prepare for the wide range of cultures, abilities, and talents they will meet in any given classroom, teachers must (1) be humble and recognize that they have much to learn from their students and communities; (2) approach teaching always with a sense of inquiry, framing questions about students' needs to guide their teaching; and (3) be willing to share their stories (p. xvi). In Sections I and II, we shared strategies to help you understand the complex nature of diversity and to recognize how much you can learn from your future students. We also shared stories and strategies that help us build and sustain our own classroom ecosystems.

The third section focuses on Delpit's second key ingredient: inquiry. Inquiry is the fountain from which culturally responsive pedagogy and content-rich curriculum spring. However, we must offer a caveat. Unlike the preceding pedagogical step-by-step strategies and assignments, which appear to be neat and tidy, inquiry can be frustrating, circuitous, and messy. According to Ruth Shagoury Hubbard and Brenda Miller Power (2003), "Teachers just beginning their own classroom research often feel overwhelmed; there is so much to study in their classrooms that they wonder how other teachers have known to start" (p. 2). With that said, the rewards of inquiry are great.

This section provides the opportunity to practice classroom research before you teach and lays an important foundation for your future professional life. Teachers who approach classrooms as ecosystems to be studied are more apt to see themselves as agents of change, creators of curriculum, and facilitators of environments that are synergistic and dynamic rather than static and uniform (see Figure III.1). Starting research early in your career may also allay those initial feelings of anxiety and of being overwhelmed that Hubbard and Power identify with teacher research.

Many of the strategies in this section may be used at different times throughout the inquiry process—but it is essential to develop your "overarching question" early on so you can revise it as you proceed. Each strategy in this section is designed to facilitate and model inquiry perspectives and processes for understanding classroom ecosystem dynamics and the features of a culturally responsive classroom.

The strategies in this section are organized into three subsections. First, Strategy 23, "Multi-Genre Inquiry Project (MGIP): Sharing the Process and Results of Inquiry," introduces the format for reporting the results of your inquiry/research. You may want to think of the MGIP guidelines as a checklist for your research, a rubric of sorts. The MGIP guidelines also highlight the tools and activities that you will use for your inquiry, which are described in more depth in the second subsection, which includes Strategies 24–31. The final subsection, Strategy 32, "Processing Classroom Inquiry," will help you to think in more depth about the field notes you gathered.

Suggestion Box

Before beginning your research, you may want to read Chapter 2 in *Pedagogy of the Oppressed*, by Paulo Freire (1993), and the article, "First Steps for Reaching and Teaching Diverse Populations: The Classroom Ecosystem and Transactional Literary Theory," by Mary Bellucci Buckelew (2009).

Figure III.1   The Classroom Ecosystem: Interdependent, Multidimensional, Transformative

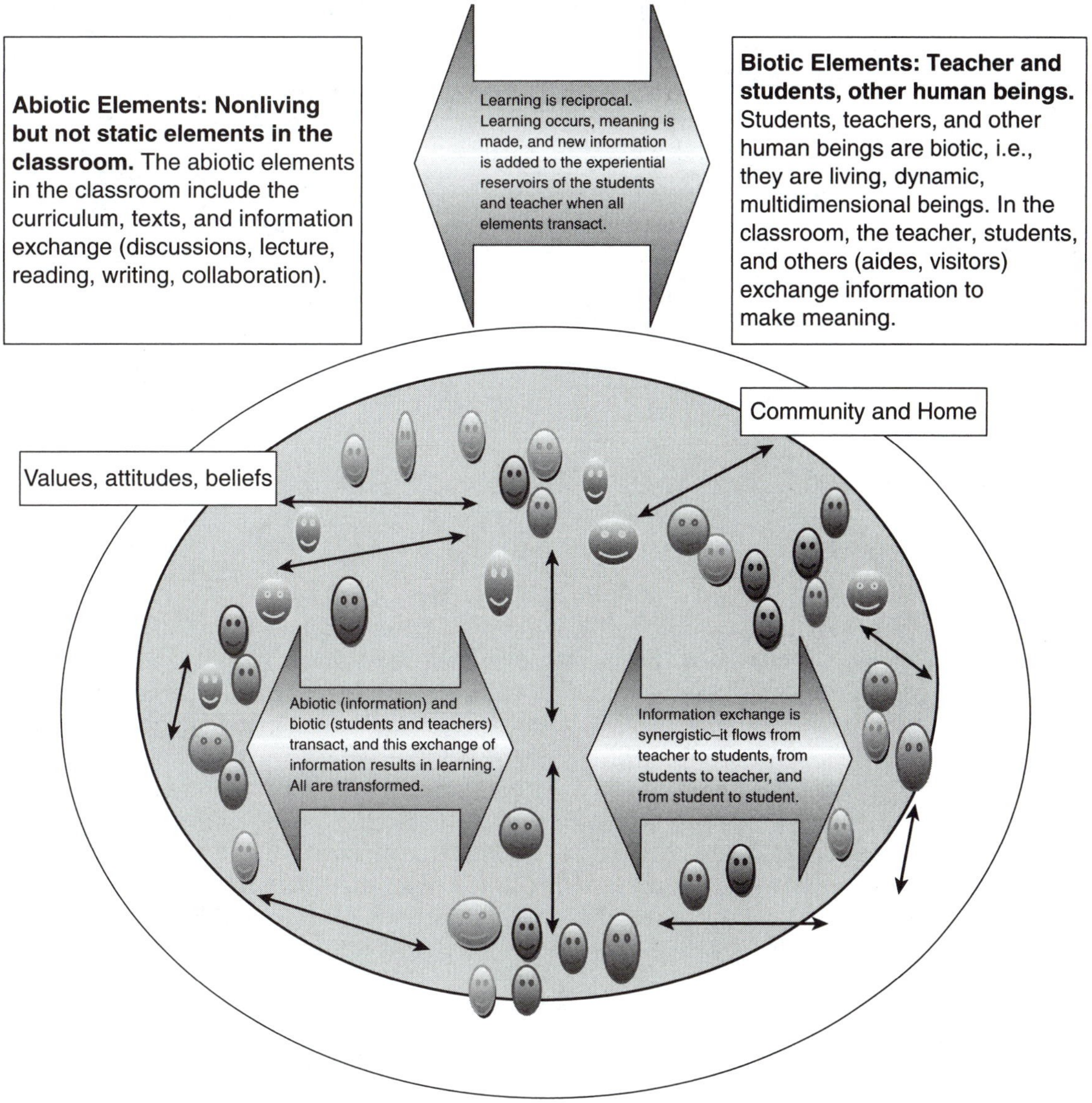

Abiotic Elements: Nonliving but not static elements in the classroom. The abiotic elements in the classroom include the curriculum, texts, and information exchange (discussions, lecture, reading, writing, collaboration).

Learning is reciprocal. Learning occurs, meaning is made, and new information is added to the experiential reservoirs of the students and teacher when all elements transact.

Biotic Elements: Teacher and students, other human beings. Students, teachers, and other human beings are biotic, i.e., they are living, dynamic, multidimensional beings. In the classroom, the teacher, students, and others (aides, visitors) exchange information to make meaning.

Community and Home

Values, attitudes, beliefs

Abiotic (information) and biotic (students and teachers) transact, and this exchange of information results in learning. All are transformed.

Information exchange is synergistic–it flows from teacher to students, from students to teacher, and from student to student.

Classroom Ecosystem: These are the individuals in the classroom having learning experiences/transactions that enter the linguistic/experiential reservoir where these new experiences/transactions encounter, mix, or conflict with what's already there from home and the community/outside. All arrows are double-headed because the individuals have to deal with input from all elements (home, community; values, atitudes, and beliefs; other students, teachers) and make meaning, which is combined with preexisting experiences and also flows outward.

Multi-Genre Inquiry Project (MGIP)

Sharing the Process and Results of Inquiry

Strategy 23

RATIONALE

As Ruth Shagoury Hubbard and Brenda Miller Power (2003) note, classroom research is necessarily messy, not neat and tidy, and even veteran teachers often find themselves overwhelmed. The multi-genre inquiry project (MGIP) format is designed as a vessel for making the process of inquiry and the final product or paper—whether paper or digital—more manageable, which is one of the reasons that the guidelines are presented here at the beginning of Section III.

The MGIP gives form and function to the various facets of this inquiry process. It intentionally reorganizes the experience so that material is not in chronological order, i.e., not in the order that activities were completed. Instead, it creates a meaningful order for the reader, foregrounding *what* was learned rather than how and when it was learned. Once you have reviewed the MGIP guidelines, you are ready to move on to Activities 24 through 32, which give step-by-step directions for each research component of the MGIP.

NOTE TO INSTRUCTOR

We suggest introducing the MGIP guidelines early in the semester so that students have time to think about what they want to research as they observe, read, and discuss. Introducing the guidelines early also gives students a chance to change their topics, which frequently happens once they start classroom observations. In addition, we suggest conducting workshops throughout the process so that students can share the sections of their MGIP with each other and with you. The workshops also help students to stay focused.

Samples of student work for the MGIP are provided throughout Section III, but you may want to access and print a completed version of the MGIP before you review the guidelines below. You may also want to ask students to visit the companion website (**http://www.sagepub.com/buckelew**) and read or print their own copies.

STEP-BY-STEP INSTRUCTIONS

1. Read the Guidelines for a Multi-Genre Inquiry Project below.

2. Review each section as a class.

3. Ask questions in class or online.

GUIDELINES FOR A MULTI-GENRE INQUIRY PROJECT

Throughout the semester, you will be required to bring sections of the MGIP to class for workshops or submit them for online workshops.

1. **Cover:** The cover identifies your topic and should visually illustrate something about the focus of your inquiry. Include your name, the date, your instructor's name, and the course number on the lower right hand corner of the cover.

2. **Table of Contents:** The table of contents lists the headings for each section and the page numbers. The following sections will serve as your table of contents' headings.

3. **Rationale:** Your rationale should reveal why you pursued your overarching question (1–4 double-spaced pages). Step-by-step instructions for writing a rationale can be found in Strategy 26.

4. **Research—Data and Analysis:** This section includes your primary and secondary sources and your analysis of each.

   a. **Double-Entry Notebook:** Include 2–4 pages of thick description and thick interpretation from your double-entry notebook. Include a reflection piece on how your double-entry notebook informed your thinking about your overarching question/topic (1–3 double-spaced pages). See Strategy 24 for specific instructions for setting up a double-entry notebook and what to include.

   b. **Interview With Teacher/Other Professional:** Include questions and answers from the interview. These questions are based on the research that you did for your overarching question, which includes your FAQs and classroom observations. Write up the interview in an informational essay or in a question-and-answer format. Use 2–3 direct quotations from the teacher in your write-up (2–3 double-spaced pages). Make sure to include quotations from the interview in your FAQs. See Strategy 28 for specific interview instructions.

   c. **Frequently Asked Questions (FAQs):** (Minimum of 8 questions and answers) Write and answer FAQs regarding your inquiry in which you address a variety of issues surrounding your overarching question. These questions and answers should provide pertinent information for anyone interested in your topic. Weave in theory, interviews with experts (teachers, educators, theorists) in the field, thick description/interpretation from your classroom observations, and other pertinent quotations that support your answers. You will also have the opportunity to brainstorm FAQs in class and visit the library to do online and text-based research so that you can answer your questions in the most informed manner. Include quotations/citations in APA format unless instructed to do otherwise. These quotations should support your answers (minimum 6–8 double-spaced pages). See Strategy 27 for FAQs instructions.

5. **Case Study:** (Optional) The case study is dependent on the type of field experience that accompanies your course and your own overarching question. If you choose to include a case study, it should incorporate Strategy 29, "The Yin and Yang of Resilience," and analysis in light of your overarching question.

6. **Findings—Looking Back/Looking Ahead:**
   a. What did you learn through this experience that begins to answer your question, and how will these findings inform your teaching?
   b. What new questions did this inquiry raise that you should keep in mind in your own teaching?
   c. Looking back on the steps, stages, and activities in this process, describe how this inquiry experience changed your way of seeing the classroom ecosystem and your understanding of reaching and teaching students. Use substantive and illustrative examples from your inquiry experience (4–8 double-spaced pages).

7. **Citations:** All citations should be written in APA format unless instructed to do otherwise.

Include the Following Appendices:

E-mail: Include a copy of the e-mail or letter that you sent to your host teacher or other professional requesting an interview.

Follow-Up Thank You: Include the follow-up thank you e-mail to the teacher/educator that you interviewed (e-mail copy/photocopy).

Professional Biography: Include a biography of the teacher/professional you interviewed. Make sure to cite where you found this information. Was it on the teacher's website, or did you solicit the information during the interview? If the latter, make sure you have permission to use this information in your paper (a paragraph or two for the bio).

Suggestion Box

If you are interested in learning more about the different types of multi-genre papers/projects, you might want to read the following books:
Putz, M. (2006). *A teacher's guide to the multigenre research project.* Portsmouth, NH: Heinemann.

Romano, T. (2000). *Blending genre, altering style: Writing the multigenre paper.* Portsmouth, NH: Boynton/Cook.

For additional information on teacher research or case studies, read the following:
Bardine, B. (n.d.). *Research to practice: "Teacher research: Getting started."* Available at http://literacy.kent.edu/Oasis/Pubs/0200-20.html.

If you choose to do a case study, you may want to read the following article:
Baxter, P., & Jack, S. (2008). Qualitative case study methodology: Study design and implementation for novice researchers. *The Qualitative Report, 13*(4), 544–559. Available at http://www.nova.edu/ssss/QR/QR13-4/baxter.pdf.

Double-Entry Inquiry Notebook

From Seeing to Meaning

Strategy 24

The basic tool for capturing your classroom observations, questions, reflections, and research is a double-entry notebook, hard copy or electronic. (You were introduced to a version of the double-entry notebook, or journal, in Section I, Strategy 10.) In addition to recording your thick description (detailed observation) and thick interpretation (analysis of observations), your notebook will help you to discover, develop, and subsequently explore your overarching inquiry question, which is detailed in Strategy 25. For classroom observations, you will need to set up your double-entry format in such a way that you record as much detail (thick description) as possible on one page before trying to interpret and analyze (thick interpretation) on the opposite of the page. For reflections and reactions to your readings, the double-entry format is essentially the same; however, on one page you may simply write a quotation from a particular reading, and on the other side react, respond, and reflect on the quotation in light of your inquiry topic/question. If field experience is an integral part of your inquiry, be sure to try Strategies 29, 30, and 31 as part of the process. (See the sample excerpt of a double-entry notebook at the end of this next section.)

FIELD-BASED THICK DESCRIPTION AND THICK INTERPRETATION—DEFINED

Thick description is essential to inquiry because it forces you to pay attention to details, great and small. While a classroom may look familiar to you because of your own years as a student, thick description forces you to pay attention so that you're seeing a classroom and a particular group as if for the first time. Thick description requires that you notice both the forest, i.e., the ecosystem in its entirety, as well as each individual tree, i.e., each student, each transaction, and any other elements contained in the ecosystem. "Thick description accurately describes objects and observed social actions (forms and features) by way of the researcher's understanding and clear description of the context under which the social actions take place" (Ponterotto, 2006, p. 543).

Recording as much detail as possible forestalls jumping to conclusions about what you're seeing by requiring that you see as much as possible first, and describe in as much detail as possible before you try to interpret. The thick description insures that you have concrete evidence for any conclusions that you ultimately reach. It also gives you enough detail in which to find patterns. You can't see a pattern in a single statement, a single conversation, a single incident, or a single example of anything. You need thick description over time to reveal patterns.

Thick interpretation assigns purpose and intentionality (functions and use) to thick description. Thick interpretation is your chance to reflect, to analyze and make meaning of what you observe. However, thick interpretation is not meant to be a process resulting in judging what you observed. Instead, it is a process for understanding a particular person, situation, or object in light of the ecosystem model; i.e., as you observe in the classroom, you will want to take into account all of the elements of the classroom ecosystem, from the bulletin board displays and materials to the teacher's pedagogy. Thick interpretation is not an act of judgment but one of making meaning in order to understand the ecosystem and the human beings who interact and exchange information within a particular setting. However, in light of your future career as a teacher, you will want to ponder in your double-entry notebook what you would like to take away from your observation, that is, what you might want to adopt, adapt, or avoid in your own classroom and why.

While the ultimate context for your foray into the ethnographer's world is the classroom ecosystem in which you are observing or teaching, the first assignment in this strategy will take place in your college classroom. The activities are designed to introduce you to the double-entry format and its purposes as well as to the field of inquiry, which will set the stage for you to become observers and reflective practitioners in your preservice classrooms and in your future classrooms. (There is an alternate homework assignment that you may want to try as well; see Observation 2.)

Excerpts From Double-Entry Notebook: (Many researchers make notes in their notebooks first and write complete thick description later.)

Date: September 3, 2011

Location: Hiland HS (Change names/identities)

Time: 8:20–9:15

Class: English 11

Thick Description:	**Thick Interpretation:**
Mr. Brown begins class by telling students how excited he is to start two new books with them. He gives a brief summary of two books, *The Lovely Bones* and *In Cold Blood*. He summarizes the plots without giving too much away—students appear attentive. He tells them they will get to choose which book they want to read. He invites students to come up and take the books back to their desks so that they can browse both of them. Students take the books back to their desks and appear to be engaged as noted by the fact that they open the books and are reading. They must choose by the end of the period.	Since I've observed this class before, I know they are usually not very interested in reading or writing even though Mr. Brown is very enthusiastic. I think allowing them choice in the text will make them more motivated to read. Since they make their choice based on their personal interests, they should be able to relate to the book and make meaningful connections to it. This will not only motivate them to do the reading, but they will also find more meaning and value in its content. Note: Ask Mr. Brown if he noticed more engagement because students chose their own books.

Note to Instructor

Section III begins with strategies you can implement in your own classroom to introduce students to the double-entry notebook. The first classroom strategy requires that students bring personal items to class such as photographs, jewelry, or awards—any mementos that are important to them. While students often have such items in their knapsacks or pocketbooks, you may want to remind them during the class period before this activity to bring a few objects to class.

Step-by-Step Instructions

Observation 1: Observing an Object

1. Select a notebook, either hard copy or electronic, in which to record your observations (thick description) and reflections (thick interpretation); however, be sure to check with your instructor before bringing your laptop into the classroom setting.

2. Reserve one side of the page or text for thick description and the other side or opposite page for thick interpretation.

3. Bring four objects to class. These objects should be important to you or illustrate something about you.

4. Pair up with someone in class.

5. Trade at least two items. Do not explain the meaning of the objects to each other, i.e., there should be no talking until both entries are complete.

6. Record thick description: On one side of your notebook or page, write a thick description of your partner's items. Include as many details as possible.

7. Record thick interpretation: On the other side of your notebook, write your initial thick interpretation. What can you infer about your partner from the objects? What are you wondering about?

8. Develop a list of possible interview questions (to ask your partner) based on your thick interpretation.

9. Interview your partner.

10. Jot down notes as you interview.

11. Write a reflection on your initial analyses of your partner's artifacts and the subsequent interview. What surprised you about your partner? About your initial thick interpretation? Your process?

12. Pair-share with partner: Discuss how your thick description, initial thick interpretation, interviewing, and final analysis might inform your classroom ecosystem observations.

13. What questions does this raise for you? Record them now.

14. Place in your professional portfolio.

OBSERVATION 2: OBSERVING A FAMILIAR PLACE

1. Thick description: Begin by sketching your roommate's or friend's bedroom. Show the location and placement of objects, pictures, posters, and anything else that will paint a clear picture for someone who is unfamiliar with the room.

2. Thick interpretation: Write a thick interpretation based on your thick description.

3. Develop interview questions.

4. Interview your roommate or friend.

5. Reflect on your initial analyses of your roommate's/friend's artifacts and subsequent interview.

6. Bring this material to class.

7. Pair-share with partner in class. Discuss how your thick description/interpretation, interview, and final analysis might inform your classroom ecosystem observations.

8. Reflect with your partner on what you learned from the interview.

9. Discuss as a whole group.

10. What questions does this raise for you? Record them now.

11. Place your homework assignment in your professional portfolio.

OBSERVATION 3: OBSERVING THE CLASSROOM ENVIRONMENT

1. Review sample double-entry pages at the end of this strategy.

2. Record date, time, and location (coded) of observation in your double-entry notebook on the thick description side of the page. Remember to change the names of anyone being observed as well as the actual location. Keep a code record for your purposes.

3. Thick description: Sketch the classroom, including the arrangement of furniture, wall hangings, bulletin board, language on posters, classroom rules, and anything else that will illustrate the physical aspects of the classroom ecosystem. Describe in as much detail as possible.

4. Thick interpretation of the physical aspects of the ecosystem: Analyze what you noted in your thick description. What did you notice that reveals the cultural values, attitudes, and beliefs of the classroom? Whose are they? The teacher's? The students'? Both? Neither? Is it a welcoming environment? Why or why not?

5. Record your thoughts and questions, and if possible interview the teacher regarding the physical aspects of the ecosystem.

6. Write a final reflection on what you learned and understand about this particular classroom, and how it will impact your future classroom. Also note any questions this raises.

OBSERVATION 4: OBSERVING INSTRUCTION

The questions below are designed to assist you in "seeing" and thinking about the pedagogy, materials, and curriculum used in the various classroom ecosystems in which you learn and observe.

1. Review the graphic organizer "Analysis of Culturally Responsive Classroom Practice" prior to your observation.

2. During your observation, make note of the approximate times and then percentages for each of the activities and items listed under the following categories: Classroom Instruction, Literacy, Resources, and Evaluation.

3. After completing the "Analysis" chart, write your thick interpretation in your notebook.

4. Review the following questions/topics below (a–d) before your first classroom observation.
   a. Organization: How are the activities in the lesson you are observing organized? What kinds of relationships do the activities create between student and text? Between student and student? Between student and teacher? In what directions do instruction and interaction move?
   b. Ownership: Who owns each aspect of the activity? What choices/decisions need to be made and who makes them?
   c. Acculturation: How do the activities you observe tap students' existing knowledge and cultural competence? What values and beliefs underlie the activities, particularly about teaching and learning? What attitudes do the activities foster?
   d. Learning theory: Where does this activity fall on each continuum below?

   Competitive_____Collaborative

   Mechanical_____Organic

   Atomistic_____Holistic

   Reactive_____Responsive

   Individual_____Inclusive

   Win–lose_____Win–win

5. Incorporate your observations regarding these questions in your thick description and your responses to all or some of the questions in your thick interpretation. Also note any questions this raises.

OBSERVATION 5: OBSERVING A STUDENT

Each observation strategy builds upon the previous. After describing the physical layout of the classroom and doing the thick interpretation, select a student (in conjunction with your host teacher) to observe. If possible, focus on this student for the duration of your field experience.

1. Observe the student in as many different situations as possible (from whole-class activities to small-group to individual activities) and write a thick description and a thick interpretation for each situation. Observe this individual through the ecosystem lens (relationships/interactions with materials, content, technology, seating, teacher, other students, aides, others). For instance, record his or her interactions with the teacher, other students, and the materials. You might note body language, the number of times the student raises his or her hand to respond to questions, and the student's engagement with the material. The more you observe, the more you'll understand the nature and dynamics of the particular classroom ecosystem and the experience of the student you are observing in this setting.

2. Thick interpretation: Analyze your thick descriptions of the student's transactions in the various situations.

3. Record your thoughts and write interview questions.

4. If permission is granted, interview the student and teacher.

Analysis of Culturally Responsive Classroom Practice

General Directions: Note number of minutes spent doing each activity. Assign a percentage to applicable items in the pie graph.

I. Within the category of *Classroom Instruction*, create a pie chart that reflects the percentage of time spent in	**II. Within the category of *Literacy*, create a pie chart that reflects the percentage of time spent in**
A. Independent student work	A. Independent reading in class
B. Modeling	B. Teacher reading aloud/students reading aloud
C. Scaffolding	C. Students reading in pairs or small groups
D. Conferring	D. Reading/writing workshop
E. Teacher lecture—note taking	E. Reading/writing done for homework
F. Use of pair-share	F. Response groups
G. Use of groups of 3–4	G. Pre-reading or rereading
H. Use of whole-classroom discussion	H. Worksheets—skill practice
I. Offering choice	I. Response to prompt on board
J. Shared decision making	J. Journal/freewriting
	K. Note taking
	L. Reading Log
	M. Metacognitive paper
	N. Evaluation

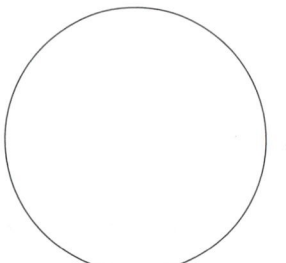 

III. Within the category of *Classroom Resources*, create a pie chart that reflects the percentage represented by each resource used in your course(s):	**IV. Within the category of *Evaluation*, create a pie chart that reflects the percentage represented by each used in your course:**
A. Use of textbook	**Summative Evaluation**
B. Use of supplementary handouts	A. Essay tests
C. Use of blackboard/overhead	B. Report writing
D. Use of visual text	C. Research: primary/secondary sources
E. Use of video	D. Presentations
F. Use of Internet/computer software	E. Multi-genre/multi-modal projects
G. Library	F. Portfolios
H. Community	G. Reflection
	Formative Evaluation
	A. Conferences
	B. Dialogue journals
	C. Pair-share
	D. Turn and talk

5. Do thick interpretation after the interview.

6. Continue observing the student in a variety of situations.

7. Write thick description and thick interpretation for each observation.

8. Note any questions this raises.

PERMISSIONS/PRIVACY

You will need to preserve the confidentiality of those you observe by changing the name of the school, teacher, and students in the data and results you write up. If you plan to present your findings in a public venue, the proper steps for securing permissions should be followed. Check with your instructor and host teacher regarding securing permission from the parents of the students you observe.

SUGGESTION BOX

For further information, read the following work:
Ponterotto, J. (2006). "Brief note on the origins, evolution, and meaning of the qualitative research concept "thick description." *The Qualitative Report, 11*(3), 538–549. Available at http://www.nova.edu/ssss/QR/QR11-3/ponterotto.pdf.

CONTENT-AREA EXTENSION

Students can use the double-entry notebook in a variety of ways, e.g., to respond to literature, art, or a historical event, or to record scientific observations and then analyze them.

ADDITIONAL APPLICATION

New and veteran teachers can apply the above activities to their classroom ecosystems, describing their own classrooms and interpreting what the arrangement and artifacts might convey to an outsider or to their own students, or they can visit each other's classroom and then meet to share the results of their observations and interpretations in their inquiry/learning communities.

Asking and Developing the Overarching Inquiry Question

Finding a Focus

RATIONALE

At the heart of classroom inquiry are questions. The question that you want to spend the semester researching will most likely come from your class readings, classroom observations, and your double-entry notebook. If you do not have a field experience component attached to the course, you may want to arrange to do some observations at a local school so that your "overarching question" is inspired by actual classroom practice. If off-campus field experience is not possible, you may want to become a participant/observer in your own college classes.

Wherever you observe, make it a habit to jot down in your double-entry notebook a list of questions that you have regarding as many elements of the ecosystem as possible (see Strategy 24: Double-Entry Inquiry Notebook).

Developing a question that is open-ended and not one that you already know the answer to is key. For instance, note the difference between "What makes differentiated instruction the best approach to a diverse classroom?" and "What is the impact of differentiated instruction in a particular content area?" A good question to pursue is a real question, i.e., one to which you don't know the answer, and an authentic question, i.e., one you really want or need to answer for yourself. If you don't really care about the answer, you won't look hard or well enough *and* you won't invest the time you need to do a good job.

The process of developing an overarching research question for your classroom inquiry should begin early in the semester so that you will have time to explore a variety of possibilities before choosing one. Inquiry is a process—a journey—and even the tangents or side roads can be as interesting as the ultimate focus or the main highway. However, in order for you to explore and finally develop a manageable question and specific research focus, you will need *time* to brainstorm, talk, and reflect with your classmates and other professionals in the field.

The goal of this strategy is to help you to think about your "wonderings" as Glenda Bissex calls them (quoted in Hubbard & Power, 1999, p. 2), and to begin shaping these wonderings into an "overarching question" that will guide your classroom research and result in a multi-genre inquiry project (MGIP; see Strategy 23 for MGIP guidelines).

NOTE TO INSTRUCTOR

Because students often find it challenging to develop an open-ended question, we have included three sample questions at the end of this strategy. You may want to spend time discussing the questions with your students.

MATERIALS

Sticky flip-chart poster paper or blank 8½ × 11 paper

STEP-BY-STEP INSTRUCTIONS

1. Read "Testing the Water With Mini-Inquiry Projects," by Jerome C. Harste and Christine Leland (1999). The article can be found at the end of this strategy.

2. Copy a sentence or two from the article that resonates with or concerns you on the left-hand page in your double-entry notebook.

3. React/respond to the quotation on the page opposite.

4. Pair-share the double entry you made.

5. Report out and discuss concerns or questions regarding inquiry.

6. Brainstorm, as a class or in pairs, questions and topics regarding "wonderings" about the classroom ecosystem and your content area.

7. Copy the questions into your notebook and add your own individual items to the list.

8. Select a topic or question that resonates for you.

9. Write your name and topic/question at the top of the sticky flip-chart poster paper and hang the posters around the room or in the hallway. Move from poster to poster, writing suggestions and questions regarding each classmate's topic. You might suggest articles or texts that are pertinent to their topics or pose further questions such as, "Have you considered . . .?"

10. Or, if space does not permit the type of response in Step 8, use a piece of 8½ × 11 paper and copy your question at the top of the paper. Place your paper on top of your desk and then move from desk to desk writing questions and comments for each of your classmates regarding their topics.

11. Once everyone has finished commenting, retrieve your own topic/question and write a reflection.

12. Review samples and definition of overarching inquiry questions in this strategy. Ask yourself, is my question specific, yet open-ended enough to be an overarching question?

13. Revise your question if needed.

14. Pair-share the current version of your question.

Sample Overarching Questions

Mary's student Katie explored the following question: "How do I foster intrinsic motivation in the high school English classroom?" John developed this question: "How is writing used in three different math classes and what role/s does it play?" Frank wrote, "Why do third graders choose the kinds of improvisational play they engage in?

LOOKING BACK/LOOKING AHEAD

What was it like to do this strategy? How might you use this strategy in your own classroom?

_____

_____

_____

_____

_____

CONTENT-AREA EXTENSIONS

K–12 students can follow the same basic steps outlined above for their research projects.

ADDITIONAL APPLICATION

New and veteran teachers can apply the above activities by framing their questions for their specific content areas; i.e., they can target their specific "wonderings" regarding diversity to their content areas, and then follow the rest of the steps.

TESTING THE WATER WITH MINI-INQUIRY PROJECTS

Jerome C. Harste and Christine Leland

Engaging teachers and undergraduate interns in mini-inquiry projects is an effective way to encourage classroom-based research. Mini-inquiry projects are just that: quick investigations of issues that get raised through professional reading, conversations, or occurrences in classrooms. Some of the questions and comments that led to mini-inquiry projects and were subsequently investigated by teachers and interns at the Center for Inquiry in Indianapolis follow:

"I think *The Witch's Broom* is too hard a book for first graders."

"I don't think children can correct their own spelling errors; if they could, they wouldn't make them in the first place."

"I think kids like books that are concrete (about things they have had experience with) rather than abstract (fantasy)."

"Are manipulatives as important for older kids as they are for the younger ones?"

"Instead of focusing on the elements of literature-characters, setting, events, main ideas-as we talk about books, will an open conversation lead to coverage of these same topics?"

"If I get Terrance to talk about the successful strategies he uses when reading, will this make him a better and more confident reader?'

Each of these musings has been the basis for a mini-inquiry project at our school. While questions might provide the most direct route into the inquiry process, statements that are shared in collaborative settings become inquiries when speaker is asked, "How do you know that?" In our combined group of teachers and interns, for example, it was one of the interns who originally commented that *The Witch's Broom* was too hard a book for first graders. Others in the group immediately asked, "How do you know that?" and "How can we find out if that's true?"

The formulation of questions leads to hypotheses and plans for gathering classroom date that will test them. More often than not, these plans are generated through collaborative discussions. In our case, teachers and interns worked together to figure out the best ways to collect appropriate data for various mini-inquiries that members of the collaborative were interested in pursuing. With concrete plans in mind, teachers and interns now saw their classrooms as places for doing research as they went about their teaching. They agreed to gather data for a specified period of time (a week, in this case) and to come together again to discuss, interpret, and analyze what they had found.

Sometimes the discussion with others led participants to revise their plans for data collection or to conclude that they had not collected enough data. In addition, we frequently found that new questions were generated before the original ones had been answered, causing inquiries to take sharp turns in new directions. In most cases, the final result was a one- or two-page write-up that was shared with the whole group.

Mini inquiry projects, we believe, have done more to establish an attitude of among our community of teachers, undergraduate interns, and university faculty than anything else we have tried. While we also engaged in some larger inquiry projects like a "sense of place" study that focused on Indianapolis, we found that these required significant investment in terms of time, travel, trips to the library, finding people to interview, and so on. Although these projects were beneficial in many ways, we felt that the mini-inquiries provided easier access to a greater variety of explorations into various aspects of teaching.

We see mini-inquiry projects as a low stress way to start messing around with inquiry. Their inherent simplicity helps to ensure that inquiry is seen as a way of life rather than as a big deal.

Philosophically, education-as-inquiry is meant to suggest that the whole of education is inquiry-everything from building curriculum according to the personal and social interests of children to seeing teaching as inquiry and ourselves as teacher-researchers. When paired with opportunities for systematic collaboration, mini-inquiries can be powerful curricular invitations that do much to support us all in becoming more reflective practitioners.

We also think that there is something to be said for the idea of venturing slowly into unknown territory. New Englanders, for example, know that the idyllic beauty of their rocky coast needs to be juxtaposed with knowledge of the frigid ocean water that can literally take one's breath away if approached without due restraint. Visitors who wish to swim there soon learn that there is less of a shock when they test the water with their toes and wade in gradually. We think there's an analogy here to teacher research. Mini-inquiries help us test the water before plunging into something that might otherwise be pretty scary. Doing teacher research (like swimming in cold water) doesn't have to leave us breathless if we start small. We might be surprised to find that once we're used to it, the new perspective is quite refreshing.

Source: Hubbard and Power, 1999. *Living the Questions* (Research Workshop).

Writing a Rationale for Your Overarching Question

Strategy 26

A rationale is defined as "a justification for doing something" (National Council of Teachers of English, 1994, p. 1). Writing the rationale for your overarching question will help you justify to yourself and your instructor that your question is one that you truly want to spend the semester exploring, and that it will benefit you as an educator and your future students. Writing your rationale gives you the opportunity to explore what you are thinking and to make meaning that you might not otherwise make.

STEP-BY-STEP INSTRUCTIONS

1. Review the feedback from your classmates regarding your initial overarching question.

2. Review your subsequent reflections.

3. List three to five things that you already know about your inquiry topic.

4. Answer the following questions about your overarching question:
   a. How is your inquiry topic related to your content area?
   b. How is your inquiry topic related to the issue of diversity?
   c. What are your professional interests in this topic?
   d. How do you personally connect to it?

5. Based on the above, write your rationale, which should include the following:
   a. A statement that describes the overarching question you wish to explore;
   b. The reason you have selected this question, i.e., why this particular question interests you personally or professionally;
   c. How your question is pertinent or connected to your reading, observations, theory, and field experience;
   d. What you hope to gain from your exploration of your overarching question.

6. Pair-share: Give feedback regarding each other's rationale.

SAMPLE RATIONALE

The following is a first draft of a rationale by Katie:

My biggest fear when I think about my future as a teacher comes in the form of questions I'll inevitably hear from a student: "What's the point? Why are we doing this?" I feel that my job as an educator is to make sure students never ask this question. I want them to feel as if everything we do has a meaning or value to their lives. If we make it relevant, they'll want to do it, right?

This desire to make my classroom content and instruction relevant led me to my overarching topic: How do teachers foster motivation in the secondary English classroom? This topic satisfied me for a period of time, but as I began exploring the intricacies of this subject, I was suddenly struck with an issue. As I explored the topic of motivation, I realized that I was really looking to explore *intrinsic* motivation. Intrinsic motivation is a student's desire to gain knowledge as driven by personal interest and perceived value of the information. So my question became, "How do teachers foster intrinsic motivation in the high school English classroom?" According to the self-determination theory, having choices and making decisions is intrinsically motivating (Eggen & Kauchak, 2006, p. 327). Accordingly, Jim Banks (1988) writes, "Students . . . are more highly motivated when the school curriculum reflects their cultures, experiences, and perspectives" (p. 2). The goal of this inquiry project is to explore the application of theories in real-life settings, specifically the English classroom, and to identify and discuss strategies to foster intrinsic motivation—strategies that I can use when I student teach.

LOOKING BACK/LOOKING AHEAD

What was it like to do this strategy? How might you use this in your own classroom?

_____

_____

_____

_____

_____

CONTENT-AREA EXTENSIONS

Whether in the physics classroom or the history classroom, students involved in research projects may follow these same steps for writing a rationale.

ADDITIONAL APPLICATION

New and veteran teachers can also follow the same steps to write a rationale for their overarching questions regarding an issue or problem in their classrooms that they wish to explore in greater depth.

Developing Frequently Asked Questions (FAQs)

Strategy 27

RATIONALE

Building background information regarding your overarching question is the foundation of your research and inquiry. The frequently asked questions (FAQs) are designed to help you build background knowledge regarding your question and to prepare you to design interview questions for a teacher or educator in the field. The interview may shape the FAQs and the FAQ research, in turn, may shape the interview questions. What distinguishes the two sets of questions is that the FAQs require you to access current and seminal research, and the interview questions should be designed so that you can explore the real-world application of your research with a veteran teacher/professional. (See the sample FAQs at the end of this strategy.)

NOTE TO INSTRUCTOR

We find that it helps students to do a whole-class brainstorming session on FAQs prior to the steps below. We usually asks a student to volunteer his or her overarching question so that the class can come up with some possible FAQs for it.

STEP-BY-STEP INSTRUCTIONS

1. Compile your own list of FAQs based on your overarching question.
2. Share your FAQs in small groups.
3. Share FAQs in a whole-group discussion.
4. Provide feedback regarding focus and possible sources for each other.

5. Homework: Begin to research your FAQs. While the FAQ research and answers do not need to be completed prior to the interview, they are meant to build your background knowledge regarding your overarching question so that you can design pertinent interview questions for your host teacher or another professional.

6. Place in your portfolio.

Looking Back/Looking Ahead

Write about your experience with this strategy—the process, product, and discussions. How might you use this strategy in your own class ecosystem?

_____

_____

_____

_____

_____

Sample FAQs for Overarching Question

Katie came up with the following overarching question (see Strategy 26): *How do we foster intrinsic motivation in the English classroom?*

FAQs

1. What is intrinsic motivation?

2. Why is intrinsic motivation important?

3. How does intrinsic motivation relate to the English classroom?

4. How does intrinsic motivation differ according to gender?

5. Does intrinsic motivation differ by race or culture?

6. How do we foster intrinsic motivation in reading and writing?

7. How do we foster intrinsic motivation when teaching vocabulary or grammar?

8. Other than with books and the RAFT method of writing, how can teachers allow students to have choices in the English classroom?

CONTENT-AREA EXTENSIONS

The FAQ strategy is one section of the MGIP (Strategy 23), but it may also be used alone, as a vehicle for building background knowledge in a particular content area. For example, the FAQs might become part of a career inquiry multi-genre project in which students build background information regarding their future careers via the FAQ strategy, or the FAQs could be part of an author study project in which students research the background and writing of a particular author and present some of their findings in the form of FAQs.

ADDITIONAL APPLICATION

New and veteran teachers can use the FAQ strategy in the same fashion as described in the Step-by-Step Instructions and Content-Area Extensions.

SUGGESTION BOX

You may want to read the following article:

Strickland, J. (2004). Just the FAQs: An alternative to teaching the research paper. *English Journal, 94*(1), 23–28. Available at http://www.jstor.org/stable/4128843.

Interviews

Designing Questions, Analyzing Answers, Making Connections

Strategy
28

RATIONALE

At the heart of inquiry is asking questions, informal (Q1) and formal (Q2). Informal and formal questions are those that shape the inquiry and "inform" the quest. *Informal questions* arise and can be asked in the context in which you are observing and can be asked during or soon after the observation. *Formal questions* are those that are shaped by the informal questions, research, observations, and a variety of data—that is, formal questions seek answers in a formal interview setting in which the interviewee will expect that you have done your research and carefully crafted your questions.

NOTE TO INSTRUCTOR

We find that it helps students to do a whole-class brainstorming session on interview questions prior to following the steps outlined further below. We usually ask a student to volunteer his or her overarching question so that the class can come up with some possible interview questions. Once students have completed the formal interview, We provide time for students to discuss their findings in preparation for analysis/thick interpretation.

INFORMAL INTERVIEW QUESTIONS (Q1)

The informal interview questions might be likened to formative assessment, i.e., just as formative assessment informs subsequent research, or writing, or reading activities, informal questions inform topic selection, the overarching question, and answers to FAQs (see Strategy 27). The informal interview questions are asked throughout the data collection process and also inform a larger piece of work like that of the multi-genre inquiry project (MGIP; see Strategy 23). As you begin your field observations, you are encouraged to list questions regarding classroom curriculum, pedagogy, management, and anything else that seems pertinent to diversity and to your growth as a reflective practitioner. Record your questions in your double-entry notebook (see Strategy 24). In the ideal setting, you will then have time to ask these formative or informal questions immediately after your observations, but if this is not possible, ask your host teacher if you can engage in an informal question-and-answer session via e-mail or phone. The informal session will help you discover topics for investigation and focus your overarching question for your MGIP. As you research your FAQs, you will note that you are able to develop more specific and insightful questions, which then become formal interview questions.

Once you have completed your interview, you will want to analyze, i.e., do the "thick interpretation" as described in Strategy 24 in light of your overarching question or research.

STEP-BY-STEP INSTRUCTIONS FOR INFORMAL INTERVIEW QUESTIONS

1. Compile your own list of informal interview questions based on your overarching question.

2. Share your interview questions in small groups.

3. Share interview questions in a whole-group discussion.

4. Provide feedback for each other regarding focus.

5. Try out some of your informal interview questions.

FORMAL INTERVIEW QUESTIONS (Q2)

For your MGIP, you will develop a set of formal interview questions for your host teacher or another professional in the field, based on your overarching question. If your course does not include a field component, you will need to seek a teacher/professional in the field to interview. Your course instructor can help facilitate this connection, or you may want to contact a former teacher.

The interview is a crucial element in classroom inquiry, and it also allows you to connect with a practitioner in the field who may be a source of future interaction and collaboration. (If you have permission to interview a student, revisit the Permissions/Privacy section in Strategy 24: Double-Entry Inquiry Notebook.) As you prepare for your interview, reference Section II of this book and review code switching (Strategy 20), as you will need to demonstrate your sense of professionalism both in securing the interview and during the interview. The following protocol activities will also help you to demonstrate and cultivate a professional image for your interview.

STEP-BY-STEP INSTRUCTIONS FOR FORMAL INTERVIEW QUESTIONS

1. Compile your own list of formal interview questions based on your overarching question and your research/FAQs.

2. Share your interview questions in small groups.

3. Share interview questions in a whole-group discussion.

4. Provide feedback for each other regarding focus.

5. Narrow your formal interview questions.

6. Conduct interview.

7. Analyze interview in light of your research/overarching question.

8. Place in portfolio.

LOOKING BACK/LOOKING AHEAD

What was it like to do the above activities? How might you use this strategy in your own classroom?

_____

_____

_____

_____

_____

NOTE TO INSTRUCTOR

Before sharing the following interview protocols, model an interview with a student or a colleague and ask the class to deconstruct what you did. After the modeling session, review the following protocols with students.

PROTOCOLS FOR INTERVIEWS (PRE, DURING, AND POST)

While much of the following may appear obvious and come naturally, it is wise to practice the art of interview etiquette. Pair up and do improvisations of each of the following protocols. One student plays the host teacher/professional and the other plays the student/interviewer. The pre-interview protocol is known as HOLA and is used when you make initial contact with the interviewee for the formal interview. This is followed by the during-interview protocol, LAFTR, and finally, the post-interview, THANK.

STEP-BY-STEP INSTRUCTIONS FOR CONDUCTING INTERVIEWS

Pre-interview protocol (HOLA):

1. H=Hello/Greeting: Greet the interviewee and introduce yourself. Acknowledge that you are grateful for the host teacher/professional's willingness to meet with you and be interviewed.

2. O=Observe: Observe the interviewee for a few seconds. Rather than diving into the interview, pause, step back after introductions, and

3. L=Listen: Allow teacher/professional to fill in the space after the introductions. Whether or not anything is said, you then

4. A=Acknowledge: Acknowledge teacher's reply and thank teacher again for agreeing to be interviewed.

During the interview, employ the following strategies (LAFTR):

1. **LA**=Listen Actively: Pay attention to what and how the interviewee responds. Demonstrate that you're listening via body language (eyebrow raises, nods, smiles, note taking).

2. **F**=Flexibility: Demonstrate your flexibility. If interviewee looks unsure, rephrase question; check for comprehension.

3. **T**=Time: Allow enough time for flexibility. Don't let prewritten questions restrain you from following an unexpected path.

4. **R**=Record: Write or record important information. If you're recording the interview using a tape or digital recorder, make sure that you have permission.

Post-interview etiquette (THANK):

1. **T**=Thank interviewee for granting the interview.

2. **H**=Handshake: Shake hands with the interviewee, if appropriate.

3. **A**=Ask if you may contact the interviewee with further questions. Ask for the person's preferred medium (e-mail or phone) for contact.

4. **N**=Note: Send a follow-up thank you note or e-mail (proofreading it first).

5. **K**=Knowledge: Analyze and synthesize, i.e., do the "thick interpretation" of your interview notes/transcript (see Strategy 24).

LOOKING BACK/LOOKING AHEAD

What was it like to do the above activities? How might you use them in your own classroom?

_____

_____

_____

_____

_____

CONTENT-AREA EXTENSIONS

Teachers may want to share Q1 and Q2 strategies as well as the protocols with students who are involved in research that requires interviewing subjects. This strategy also works well in ELL classrooms to illustrate for students the general rules of interaction in U.S. culture.

ADDITIONAL APPLICATION

New and veteran teachers can use the Q1 and Q2 strategies in their own classroom inquiry to interview students or colleagues regarding classroom observations, pedagogy, and theory.

Perspective Taking in the Ecosystem Classroom

The Yin and Yang of Resilience

This strategy recognizes that the world in which we live is composed of individuals engaged in dynamic relationships with others and with their environments. In other words, though any individual can be viewed summatively—as discrete and separate from others—at any given moment, lived reality is rarely that static or singular, so while the summative view is sometimes necessary, it is rarely sufficient for educators' purposes.

Recent theory supports this more interactive, dynamic view of human development. Positing a "transactional-ecological model," developmental theorists suggest that personality is a "self-righting mechanism engaged in active, ongoing adaptation to its environment" virtually all the time (Benard, 1991, p. 3). In other words, seeing a student as an individual is sometimes useful, but seeing a student as interacting with others and with the environment provides a richer—and more realistic—understanding on which to base teaching and learning experiences.

The concept of *resilience* helps structure this kind of useful perspective taking. Originating in research on at-risk populations, resilience was the unexpected quality identified in children and adolescents who did not fall victim to the risk factors in their lives. As researchers learned more about these children, they began to recognize "protective factors" in both the individual children and their particular situations that made them successful despite their circumstances. They realized, too, that these factors can be developed—and nurtured—to create more positive, effective individuals and more supportive, sustainable systems.

The protective factors likely to create a resilient individual are these:

- Social competence—characterized by responsiveness, flexibility, empathy, caring, effective communication skills, sense of humor, and easy temperament

- Problem-solving skills, both cognitive and social

- Autonomy—characterized by a sense of independence, self-discipline, and the ability to be purposeful, responsible, and self-directed; an internal locus of control

- Good physical health

The systemic features—of school, home, and community settings—necessary to foster these qualities are these:

- Caring and support from at least some others in the environment

- High expectations with accompanying support

- Opportunities for meaningful participation

In other words, students become more resilient—develop attributes in the crucial categories—not solely from individual bootstrap efforts, but also in relationships with others and in sustainable settings that support their attempts. Teachers cannot control the family or community contexts of students' lives, but they can control the classroom and school contexts—i.e., ecosystems—on which we focus here.

Once the systemic features that foster resilience are in place in a school setting, their impact is cyclical.

- First, classroom culture/environment teaches students how to see themselves.

- Then, students see themselves determines how they see and treat others.

- Then, students see and treat others teaches those others how to respond in return.

- Finally, students respond to each other creates and sustains the environment.

This means the classroom culture must model desirable, effective ways to be, i.e., ways to develop the attributes of resilience. For example, a student sees the teacher and other students being responsive, caring, empathetic, flexible, and so on, so the student begins to value and imitate those behaviors, providing care and support for others, and prompting care and support in return. It is not just the teacher who builds relationships with each student. It is also each student building relationships with peers. The older the students, the more important such positive peer support becomes.

Before using this strategy as an inquiry tool, you will use it to analyze your own experience in resilience terms. Then you will be able to use it more effectively in your inquiry setting.

STEP-BY-STEP INSTRUCTIONS

PART 1

1. Using the Yin-Yang diagram provided, put yourself in the central circle. Decide whether you will define "Family" as immediate or extended. Identify at least two "Communities" important to you. These should include a classroom, and may also include a school, dorm, fraternity or sorority, or religious group—any setting(s) in which you interact regularly.

2. Use the Yin-Yang Resilience Analysis section below to code each aspect of your diagram. When considering the classroom setting, be sure to think about these aspects of the classroom: curriculum; materials; assessment; rules and procedures; values, attitudes, and beliefs.

3. On a separate sheet of paper, describe what you get from and give back to each of the identified settings based on the analysis chart you completed.

4. Share your diagram with a partner. Discuss needs that are met and unmet in these transactions.

5. Prepare for class discussion: What behaviors (verbal and nonverbal), habits, and practices would you expect to see in a relationship that provides caring and support for each individual? That holds high expectations for each person? That provides opportunities for meaningful participation by each one?

6. Prepare a blank diagram for use in your field research setting.

See below for diagram and analysis sheet.

PART 2 (OPTIONAL—FOR USE IN YOUR FIELD SETTING)

1. Explain this assignment to the teacher in your field experience or student teaching setting. Together, identify a student of interest who can become the focus of your resilience analysis.

2. Do the resilience analysis for the *individual* and *classroom* circles of the yin-yang diagram. Do the *family* circle only if your cooperating teacher considers that appropriate.

3. On a separate sheet of paper, describe what your student of interest gets from and gives back to each of the identified settings. Identify needs met and unmet in this student's environments.

4. Prepare for class discussion: What behaviors (verbal and nonverbal), habits, and practices did you see in your field experience classroom that provide caring and support for your student of interest? That hold high expectations for that student? That provide opportunities for meaningful participation by that student? What else did you notice that has implications for you as a teacher?

YIN-YANG RESILIENCE ANALYSIS

RISK FACTORS

List corresponding numbers in the shaded area of each circle on the analysis chart (see Figure 29.1 on page 125).

Individual

1. Sense of alienation from others

2. Current antisocial behavior, acting out

3. Little commitment to school

4. Academic failure

5. History of antisocial behavior

6. Favorable attitude toward substance abuse, smoking, other hazardous behavior

7. Mental health issues

Family

8. Absence of strong bond with any family member

9. Family management problems

10. Family violence

11. Economic and social deprivation

12. Parental drug use or other hazardous behavior

13. Parental mental health issues

Community(ies)

14. Absence of strong friendships with peers

15. Friends, other role models, or community norms favoring antisocial behavior

16. Friends, other role models, or community norms favoring little commitment to school/academic success

17. Friends, other role models, or community norms favoring drug use or other hazardous behaviors

18. Low neighborhood attachment, community disorganization

19. Transitions, instability, mobility

PROTECTIVE FACTORS

List corresponding letters in the unshaded area of each circle on the analysis chart (see Figure 29.1).

Individual

A. Autonomy, internal locus of control
B. Social competence
C. Problem-solving skills, cognitive and/or social
D. Sense of humor
E. Good physical health
F. High self-esteem
G. Easy temperament
H. Bonded to school

Family

A. High expectations for everyone
B. Opportunities for meaningful participation by everyone
C. Supportive, consistent communication among members
D. Parental stability, emotional and situational
E. Economic stability

F. Sibling support
G. Parental disapproval of drug use and other hazardous behavior
H. Parents model positive values, attitudes, beliefs, and behaviors

Community(ies)

A. High expectations for everyone
B. Opportunities for meaningful participation by everyone
C. Positive participatory school climate
D. Friends with positive attitudes toward school and academic achievement
E. Supportive, caring relationship with an adult nonfamily member
F. Positive adult role models
G. Neighborhood attachment/cohesion
H. Social norms opposing drug use and other hazardous behavior

Figure 29.1   Yin-Yang Resilience Analysis Template

Directions: From the following code sheet: 1) place the numbers of the respective *risk* factors that apply for this individual in the *shaded* side of each circle and 2) place the letters of the respective *protective* factors that apply for this individual in the *white* side of the circle.

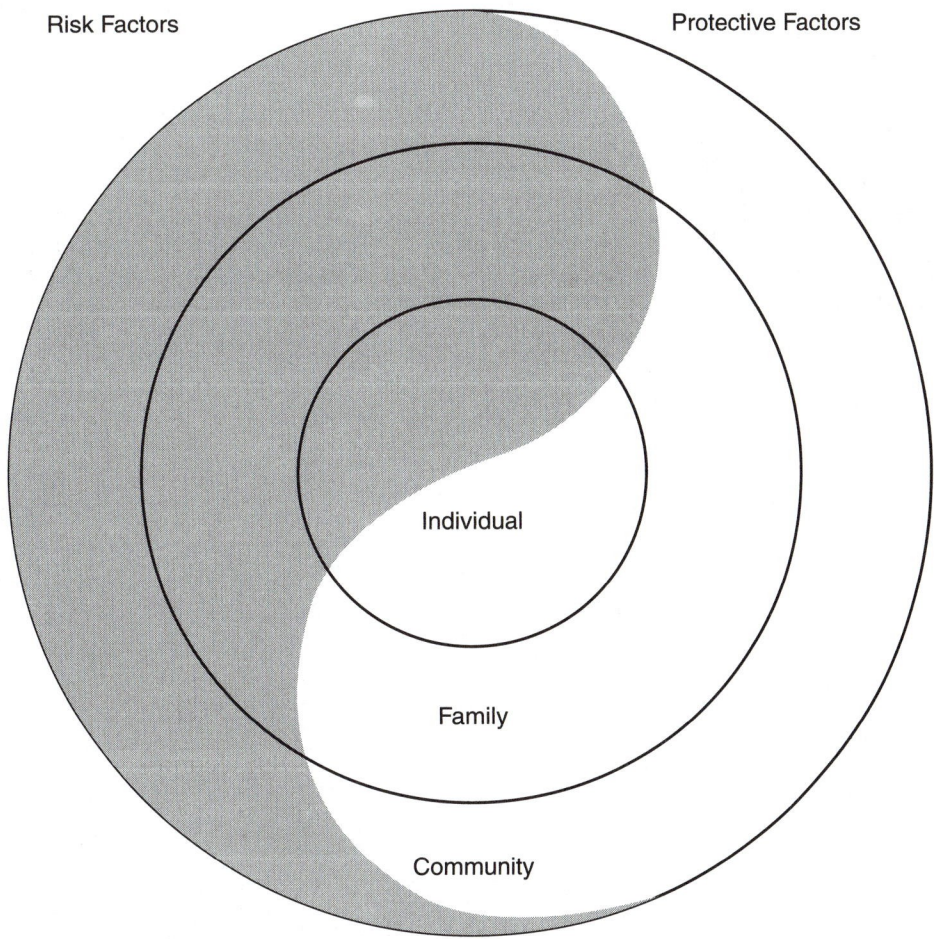

Risk Factors

Protective Factors

Individual

Family

Community

Source: Adapted from the Shippensburg University Model for Developing Community-Based Prevention, by Dr. Anne Gero, 1986.

LOOKING BACK/LOOKING AHEAD

What was it like to do this strategy? How might you use this strategy in your own classroom?

_____

_____

_____

_____

_____

ADDITIONAL APPLICATION

This strategy helps new and veteran teachers to view students through the lens of resilience in order to create and implement activities that foster resilience.

SUGGESTION BOX

If you are interested in reading more about resiliency, see the following article:
Benard, B. (1991). The foundations of the resiliency framework: From research to practice. In N. Henderson (Ed.), *Resiliency in action*. Available at http://www.resiliency .com/htm/research.htm.

What They Think They're Doing

Strategy 30

Withholding Judgment
in Order to Understand

From the time children are old enough to understand, they learn to move through the world, judging as they go: Are people they meet good or bad? Are others' ideas right or wrong? Is their behavior moral or immoral? By the time most students reach college, many of their perceptions and opinions have generalized into apparent facts. Students may think they know, for example, what counts as a family, how families should function, what parents owe their children, and what children owe their parents. For some, that might mean only a two-parent household where mother and father support all the aspirations and desires of their children is good or right. So when they meet someone from a single-parent home, where he or she had to help care for siblings or work for spending money, they doubt that classmate had a proper upbringing. (This holds true for most hot-button social issues, explaining what makes them so "hot.")

The same applies to perceptions and beliefs about education. What counts as a good school, good teaching, or good students are matters of fact to some students, and these "facts" may not be amenable to discussion—let alone change—in the course of regular assigned reading and class discussion.

This habit of judging serves all of us well—even keeps us safe—in some settings, but it is counterproductive for teachers engaged in action research. The primary goal of such research, like that of other qualitative researchers, is to answer Geertz's (1973) question, "What the devil do they think they're doing?" when people seem to behave in ways the researcher either doesn't approve of or doesn't recognize. In other words, what matters is not what the researcher thinks is going on. What matters is what the subjects of the research think they are doing.

This was brought home to Andrea most dramatically when, in an Amish classroom she was studying, a fifth grader's "nature study report" that began, *"Forget me knot, name given to plants of the genus Myosotis, belonging to the family Boraginaceae (q.v.). They are found in temperate zones in all parts of the world. A number of species are common in ditches and damp meadows of the U.S.,"* and continued exactly that way, received an A. The student had clearly copied word-for-word from the classroom encyclopedia, without even noting the source. How could that teacher condone plagiarism? Andrea wondered. What did she think she was doing?

After trying hard to think *with* instead of *against* the teacher, Andrea looked at other student work in other grades and subjects to determine whether there was a pattern of practice that might help her understand what she was seeing. Discovering consistent, literal, limited reading and writing in this one-room Amish school, she realized there had to be both reason and meaning in what this teacher did so consistently. But what did she think she was teaching through these assignments and these criteria?

Finally, Andrea realized that finding and copying the necessary information was, in the teacher's view, the most efficient, most reliable way to report the facts. Why waste time trying to reframe the information in a student's own words? In addition, the student made no attempt to pretend those were her words. No one did. In fact, that would have been antithetical to the community's belief in humility, in not being proud or showing off. So while Andrea's initial shock came from having her own values, attitudes, and beliefs challenged by what she saw, her *learning* came from letting go of the fault-finding, oppositional game she was programmed to play and replacing it with the inquiry mind-set that provided insight into what she was seeing. This does not mean plagiarism suddenly became an acceptable practice for all classrooms everywhere. Rather, it exemplified and reinforced the understanding that best practice does not mean universally acceptable practice. Best practice is best defined in terms of classroom culture and context—in terms of the values, attitudes, and beliefs not of researchers, but of participants.

When beginning your own observations or research, you may not have time to search for patterns, and this is when your informal and formal interview questions (Strategy 28) become invaluable in understanding and analyzing (thick interpretation) what you are studying.

This strategy is designed to help you achieve the flexibility of mind required for honest inquiry. It structures the opportunity to practice thinking *with* rather than *against* the people in your research setting. Applicable to thick interpretation (Strategy 24) and to interviewing (Strategy 28), this strategy can become your default perspective, helping you think with instead of against classmates and colleagues as well as with inquiry subjects, making the classroom ecosystem a more supportive, sustainable space.

NOTE TO INSTRUCTOR

Have students select a double-entry observation about which they have questions.

STEP-BY-STEP INSTRUCTIONS

1. Small-group work: Using the double-entry observation you chose, think *with* the people involved. What's right about what they've done? Why might they have done what they did? What might they value in this work or this story? Now list the questions you would ask of the teacher or students involved if you could interview them.

2. Prepare for class discussion: To what extent was this easy? Difficult? What made it that way?

3. Choose a story that clings from your research setting or double-entry notebook (Strategy 24). Write the thick description version, including all significant descriptive details. Next, write one paragraph finding fault with what happened and one paragraph inquiring about or thinking *with* the people involved. Conclude by writing several paragraphs in which you analyze the potentially positive and potentially negative impact of what you saw on the students and classroom community you observed. From this thinking, develop interview questions you want to ask of the people involved.

LOOKING BACK/LOOKING AHEAD

What was it like to do this strategy? How might you use "What They Think They're Doing" in your own classroom?

_____

_____

_____

_____

_____

CONTENT-AREA EXTENSIONS

This strategy can be used in Language Arts, Social Studies, or Foreign Language classes whenever students are learning about a cultural practice they find strange or off-putting, or simply do not understand. It can also be used to understand characters—or real people—about whom they read.

ADDITIONAL APPLICATION

If you are a new or veteran teacher, think against/think with people involved in incidents in your professional experience. Take your write-up to induction program, department, or grade-level meetings where they can be processed by the group using a think tank protocol.

SUGGESTION BOX

For an example of an ethnographic study that further illuminates the thinking with and thinking against idea, you might want to read "Deep Play: Notes on the Balinese Cockfight," in the following book:

Geertz, C. (1973). _The interpretation of cultures_. New York: Perseus. Excerpt available at http://www.si.umich.edu/~rfrost/courses/MatCult/content/Geertz.pdf.

A-List/B-List

Getting Beyond Stereotypes in the Field

Strategy
31

If you worked through the strategies in Section II, you learned to get beyond stereotypes of yourself and your classmates. However, you also need to get beyond stereotypes when looking at teachers and students in your inquiry project. Because it is crucial that researchers not see all members of any group as interchangeable, you need to know as much about the individuals you're observing as possible. Using the A- and B-lists in this strategy will help do that by informing your overarching questions, interviews, and field observations.

Consider this example:

A student begins with the question, "What happens when a white teacher uses literature by a black author in an all-white class?" He or she plans to observe a teacher who is doing this, and to interview both the teacher and some students in the class.

First, the question needs to be narrowed in A-list and B-list terms. One version of the question might be, "What happens when a middle-aged, middle-class, central Pennsylvania woman who's been teaching for 20 years teaches *Roll of Thunder, Hear My Cry*—a book by a black author about poor African Americans in rural Mississippi in 1933—to her all-white, small-town, Pennsylvania sixth graders in 2010?"

That is very different from another version of the same initial question: "What happens when *Roll of Thunder, Hear My Cry* is taught in an upscale Orange County, California, classroom by a 20-something, white male teacher who grew up in Los Angeles and went to UCLA?" Change the book to Walter Dean Myer's *Monster*—about an African American teenager accused of a crime in an urban setting in 2001—and change the class to eighth graders, and the question changes again, significantly, even if the teacher doesn't.

When researchers observe any of the classes described above, they may not know enough about who's in the room to fully understand what they are seeing. In that case, the A- and B-lists can inform the interviews of teacher and students and the analysis of observation data. (See Strategy 14 for the A-list and B-list identifiers.)

STEP-BY-STEP INSTRUCTIONS

1. Look at the first draft of your overarching question. Who and what, in A- and B-list terms, are you asking about? Revise your question to make it more specific.

2. Look at the first draft of your interview questions. What A- and B-list information about your interviewee makes a difference to your inquiry? Revise existing questions or write new ones to obtain that information.

3. When analyzing your field observation notes, ask yourself, "What A- and B-list features help explain or qualify what I'm seeing?"

ADDITIONAL APPLICATION

This strategy does not need to be changed for new or veteran teachers doing action research.

Processing Classroom Inquiry

- Don't judge a book by its cover.

- Don't jump to conclusions.

- The truth will out.

- Still waters run deep.

- Patience is a virtue.

People accustomed to microwave ovens, instant messaging, and sound-bite culture may consider these traditional adages old-fashioned, but they reflect a basic principle of effective inquiry and one with which researchers need considerable practice. While one set of student papers or one week of classroom observations might yield what looks like a lot of data—enough on which to base conclusions—in fact, that is just an introduction to the world of field experience or student teaching. Snapshot data may be intriguing, but only triangulated data yields legitimate findings.

Consider these three responses to an eighth-grade reading assignment in the Amish school alluded to in Strategy 30. The three eighth-grade boys read a basal reader story called "The Joker," in which boarding-school boys learn a predictable lesson about practical jokes. They answered the questions following the story.

Question 1: What was the joke that the boys played on Eddie Davis?
   Daniel's answer: moved the furniture into Charlie's room
   Richard's answer: moved his furniture in another room
   Davy's answer: hid his stuff

Question 2: Why did they choose Eddie to play the joke on? What does the word *gullible* mean?
   Daniel: they could make him believe things that aren't so, easily tricked
   Richard: he was afraid of Charlie easy to be tricked
   Davy: he didn't get mad at him, easily fooled

Question 3: What type of person was Dennis Conron? Use parts of the story as evidence for what you say.

Daniel: short and cheerful
Richard: cheerful looking boy
Davy: short cheerful little boy

Question 4: Do you feel Dennis could be blamed for Eddie's accident? Write a paragraph explaining your feelings on this.
Daniel: yes
Richard: yes
Davy: yes, because he did it

While the work of any one student would be interesting and would suggest certain lessons these students were learning about what counts as an acceptable written response, one student's paper would be an insufficient basis on which to draw conclusions. Looking at all the eighth-grade responses, however, several patterns emerge. It looks like (1) students use as few words as possible, (2) students don't explain their answers, and (3) students write in fragments and have little control of or concern about punctuation.

These patterns raise questions about what these students—and their teacher—may value and believe about teaching and learning: Why don't the students write at length? Is it too difficult or too much trouble? Does it take too much time that could be better spent doing something else? Is writing totally separate from reading? Why don't they worry about sentence structure and punctuation? Do they care more about content than form? Does being accurate matter more than being correct? Do they separate "reading" from "writing" and only worry about one at a time?

To answer these questions, more data is needed. Student writing done in other content areas or for other purposes should be analyzed to see if the pattern continues or changes and what that suggests about values, attitudes, and beliefs. This pattern across students in one assignment is an interesting place to begin but is itself insufficient for drawing conclusions about written work in this grade or this classroom. (The same holds true for other forms of data.)

For instance, Mary's student Sophia chose to observe John, an eighth-grade student. Sophia observed John in a variety of settings. She started out observing him in his English classroom in whole-class activities such as discussion and lecture sessions. She noted in her "thick description" (see Strategy 24) that John never volunteered during discussion and sat slumped over during the entire class period. In the next class, when students were asked to read aloud, John started coughing and the teacher excused him. Sophia then had the opportunity to observe John in the cafeteria and noted that he seemed to be a totally different person. He was surrounded by a small circle of friends, laughing, and always in conversation. When Sophia observed John in a small-group literature circle activity, she noted that he leaned forward and was actively engaged with the other four students and the content. Sophia's "thick interpretation" (see Strategy 24) sparked more questions than answers; i.e., she realized that she needed to see John in other small-group settings to discern if his level of engagement in the small group was part of a pattern.

Step-by-Step Instructions

1. Identify one category of data in your notebook, e.g., students' written response to reading questions or students' oral participation/behavior in literature circles.

2. Work with a partner; share your data. Together, look for patterns in each data set.

3. Discuss what those patterns suggest about the students' or teacher's values, attitudes, or beliefs as revealed by those patterns.

4. Record the list of tentative findings in your notebook for future consideration when more data has been collected.

CONTENT-AREA EXTENSIONS

English/Language Arts: This strategy can be used to look at anything from syntactical patterns to symbolism in works of fiction and nonfiction.

Science/Math: This strategy can be used to look for patterns in mathematical formulas/equations and scientific experiments and observations.

ADDITIONAL APPLICATION

This strategy does not need to be changed for new or veteran teachers doing inquiry/action research.

SUGGESTION BOX

For more on processing data, we recommend the following easy-to-read book: Hubbard, R. S., & Power, B. M. (2003). *The art of classroom inquiry: A handbook for teacher-researchers.* Portsmouth, NH: Heinemann.

SECTION IV

Analyzing Pedagogy for the Classroom Ecosystem

The first three sections of this book provide strategies your instructor can use—and you can do—to reach and teach everyone by getting beyond stereotypes in a course you are currently taking. The strategies in this section are designed to create, support, and sustain the classroom ecosystem of which you are currently a part while at the same time showing you, through experience, how this can be done.

Section I focused on you as an individual, developing self-awareness of your multiple identities. You articulated who you are as a person, getting beyond the labels of any one or two groups to which you belong.

Section II focused on individuals' interactions in and with other identifiable groups. You explored how these groups see and are seen by each other and learned ways to use the beyond-stereotypes approach to help individuals connect despite differences by finding personal common ground.

In Section III, you used the beyond-stereotypes lens to do inquiry in someone else's classroom. You learned the skills and strategies teacher-researchers use to help create and sustain effective classroom ecosystems with diverse populations.

Here in Section IV, you will analyze the implications of a beyond-stereotypes approach for creating your own successful classroom ecosystem no matter how apparently diverse your students may be.

This section reviews a set of current "best practice" strategies you have learned in your methods courses and might have experienced as a student. You will learn four different ways to analyze these strategies: for organization, for ownership, for acculturation, and for learning theory. Each kind of analysis will help you decide whether the strategy is culturally responsive and how it might help you create and sustain your own classroom ecosystem. Then you will apply these analyses to create your own lesson and unit plans as final projects for a course, for student teaching, or for your first professional assignment.

Popcorn (a.k.a. Quaker) Reading

Strategy 33

Quaker reading is an oral reading strategy that gets its name from the Quaker practice of speaking when you are moved to do so. (Some teachers call it "popcorn reading" because of the way different voices "pop up.") In other words, students do not read in a round-robin formation, nor do they read predetermined segments of text. Instead, everyone reads the text silently first. Each student decides which segment—a sentence, several sentences, or a paragraph—is most interesting or important to him or her. When the oral reading begins, each student reads aloud when his or her chosen portion appears. If two students start reading at the same time, that's fine. They continue to read chorally. The wait time between voices is not a problem. Instead, it is time in which the last segment read hangs in the air for continued effect and consideration.

Teachers of all grade levels and content areas like Quaker reading because after students get used to the procedure, it calls attention to how ideas sound in different voices and how pauses create emphasis or give you time to think about something you might have missed in your own reading. It also shows which ideas in a text students consider most important or most interesting, giving everyone a sense of what the text means and what matters.

ANALYSIS FOR ORGANIZATION

The following questions ask you to analyze how Quaker reading is *organized*. In other words, they ask you to look at the directions in which instruction and interaction move, the extent to which the strategy is teacher-directed or student-directed.

1. What kind of relationship does Quaker reading create between the student and the text being read?

2. What kind of relationships does Quaker reading create among the students in the classroom?

3. What kinds of relationships does Quaker reading create between the students and the teacher?

4. How do these relationships tap and validate individual students' prior knowledge and cultural experience?

5. How do these relationships help create and sustain a diverse classroom ecosystem?

Strategy 34

Literature Circles

literature circles have become one of the most commonly occurring strategies in K–12 classrooms. Whether used with literary or content-area texts, with predefined or naturally occurring student roles, with assigned or student-selected questions, with homogeneous or heterogeneous groups, with a shared text or a variety of texts, or under another name (e.g., reading response groups), these small-group discussions of what students have read share the following characteristics:

- Students sit together in small groups.
- They talk without the teacher present.
- They share their understandings, wonderings, and questions with each other.
- They decide what's happening in a text and what the text may mean.
- They share their group's thinking with other groups and with the teacher.

Teachers have adapted literature circles in so many ways because they promote more thorough understanding of text by inherently differentiating instruction to engage students more fully.

ANALYSIS FOR OWNERSHIP

The following questions ask you to analyze who "owns" the process and the content of literature circle pedagogy. They ask you to think about what choices and decisions need to be made, who makes them, and how. They highlight the many different ways this strategy can be implemented. In other words, they ask you to look at how literature circles help all students engage with the text, the content, and each other.

1. Who decides how groups are formed? Why and how might the teacher decide? Why and how might students decide? How might this decision be shared?

2. Who decides how the group discussion should be structured, i.e., what questions should be asked or topics should be covered? Why and how might the teacher decide? Why and how might the students decide? How might these decisions be shared?

3. How do these decisions tap and validate individual students' prior knowledge and cultural experience?

4. How do these decisions help create and sustain a diverse classroom ecosystem?

Save the Last Word for Me

Strategy 35

This strategy, adapted from the National School Reform Faculty version, can be used to structure literature circles or whole-class discussion. It may focus on something students have read, or it may focus on any issue, topic, or experience of interest.

After everyone has read a particular text, shared a particular experience, or identified a topic of concern, students have a few minutes to write about what they considered most interesting, most important, or most troublesome about the text, topic, or experience.

Students then move into groups of three or four (depending on how much time the teacher wants to allot for the small-group discussions). One member of the group identifies just the aspect of the text or experience he or she wrote about. The student does not say why he or she chose it. Each other member then gets one minute to respond to that idea. After all other group members have spoken, the first student gets 3 minutes to explain why he or she chose that aspect and how his or her thinking is similar to or different from that of the other group members.

The same process is repeated until everyone has had "the last word." The teacher can then ask students to share what happened in their groups in terms of content, process, or both.

Teachers like protocols like this one for several reasons. The clear, timed structure manages time most effectively. It also insures that no student dominates the discussion and no student is exempt from participating. From the student perspective, this gives everyone equal opportunity to speak and lets them know they've been heard.

ANALYSIS FOR ACCULTURATION

The following questions ask you to analyze the kind of "culture" this strategy helps to create and its relationship to whatever cultures students bring to the classroom.

1. What values and beliefs underlie "Save the Last Word for Me"? Specifically, what would a teacher who uses this strategy believe about who should be allowed to talk? About how students should listen to each other? About what counts as a valuable contribution to discussion? What kinds of thinking would this teacher value?

2. What attitudes toward other students are fostered by "Save the Last Word for Me"? What attitudes toward differences of opinion does it promote? What attitudes toward individual worth and merit does it suggest?

3. How do these values, beliefs, and attitudes tap and validate individual students' prior knowledge and cultural experience?

4. How do these values, beliefs, and attitudes help create and sustain a diverse classroom ecosystem?

Strategy 36

Rubric Protocol

Consistent with current research on the need for multiple evaluation methods, the *rubric protocol* provides a structure through which students can develop their own evaluation tools. Whether students are writing papers or doing science experiments, creating their own rubric deepens their understanding of what counts as "good work" and enhances their sense of ownership in whatever the project may be.

This protocol works best in small groups, with each group reporting their results to the whole class, perhaps to be combined into one shared rubric. Groups should meet at least twice: midway through the project to help direct ongoing work and close to completion to fine-tune the rubric and help with final revisions.

Before groups meet for the first time, the teacher reviews the assignment and provides the class with learning outcomes for the project. The teacher also models how he or she created a rubric with which students are already familiar. Then the teacher gives each group poster or large Post-it paper and asks them to identify their recorder, who will write down the results of their discussion for reporting-out purposes. Groups then identify their facilitator, who will insure that everyone has a chance to speak and that the work is done in the time allotted.

Groups begin by brainstorming all the possible items and categories for the rubric. These might include the quality of the information, its correctness, relevance, analysis, and development, which could be grouped as Content. They might include elements of text, graphics, sound, video, and organization, grouped as Design. If there is research involved, there may be a Preparation category, covering the quality and variety of sources and resources, permissions to use copyrighted material, and any outlining or storyboarding done as part of the process. If there is an oral component, aspects of Presentation like eye contact, volume, inflection, and technical proficiency might be included.

When the brainstorming is finished, the group creates a draft of their rubric using a graphic organizer. They decide on the number of points for each category and each item, and fine-tune their language as time allows. This draft is then shared with the class. After all drafts have been shared, a whole-class discussion can determine whether each group uses its own rubric or a whole-class combined version should be used.

ANALYSIS FOR LEARNING THEORY

1. Where does the rubric protocol fall on each continuum below?

   Competitive_____Collaborative

   Mechanical_____Organic

   Atomistic_____Holistic

   Reactive_____Responsive

   Individual_____Inclusive

   Win–lose_____Win–win

2. How does the rubric protocol tap and validate individual students' prior knowledge and cultural experience?

3. How might the rubric protocol help create and sustain a diverse classroom ecosystem?

Strategy 37

Graffiti Wall

This strategy sets aside part of one classroom wall—covered with brown butcher paper—as the place where students can write signed or anonymous comments or questions about what's going on in the course, classroom, school, or community. The teacher can put up the paper and let students write whatever they will (in school-appropriate language, of course). Or he or she can limit the topics and kinds of comments available. For example, the teacher can say, "This week I want to know what's happening for you in math," or "I want to know how your response groups are working," or "What's it like for you on the playground?" or "What would make the cafeteria a better place for everyone?" Or he or she can simply say, "Tell me what I need to know (about _____)."

Teachers like graffiti walls because they provide an additional means of formative assessment for both academic and social purposes without taking time away from instruction.

COMBINED ANALYSIS

Now you are ready to analyze a single strategy for all aspects of culturally responsive pedagogy to determine whether it will help you create and sustain a diverse classroom ecosystem.

ORGANIZATION

1. What kind of relationship does a graffiti wall create between the student and the text being read, the subject studied, or the topic under consideration?

2. What kind of relationships does a graffiti wall create among the students in the classroom?

3. What kinds of relationships does a graffiti wall create between the students and the teacher?

4. How do these relationships tap and validate individual students' prior knowledge and cultural experience?

5. How do these relationships help create and sustain a diverse classroom ecosystem?

Ownership

1. Who decides what should be discussed on the graffiti wall? Why and how might the teacher decide? Why and how might students decide? How might this decision be shared?

2. Who decides who gets to write on the wall and what that writing should look and sound like? Why and how might the teacher decide? Why and how might the students decide? How might these decisions be shared?

3. How do these decisions tap and validate individual students' prior knowledge and cultural experience?

4. How do these decisions help create and sustain a diverse classroom ecosystem?

Acculturation

1. What values and beliefs underlie the graffiti wall? Specifically, what would a teacher who uses this strategy believe about who should be allowed to express an opinion? About how students should listen to each other? About what counts as a valuable contribution to discussion? What kinds of thinking would this teacher value?

2. What attitudes toward other students are fostered by a graffiti wall? What attitudes toward differences of opinion does it promote? What attitudes toward individual worth and merit does it suggest?

3. How do these values, beliefs, and attitudes tap and validate individual students' prior knowledge and cultural experience?

4. How do these values, beliefs, and attitudes help create and sustain a diverse classroom ecosystem?

Learning Theory

1. Where does the graffiti wall fall on each continuum below?

Competitive_____Collaborative

Mechanical_____Organic

Atomistic_____Holistic

Reactive_____Responsive

Individual_____Inclusive

Win–lose_____Win–win

2. How does the graffiti wall tap and validate individual students' prior knowledge and cultural experience?

3. How might the graffiti wall help create and sustain a diverse classroom ecosystem?

SUGGESTION BOX

Select your favorite activities from Section I or Section II. Analyze them for their possible contribution to your own classroom ecosystem.

Culturally Responsive Curriculum

Strategy 38

RATIONALE

Perhaps the most difficult aspect of reaching and teaching diverse populations is deciding which stories to include in the curriculum, which stories to tell in the classroom. In the late 20th century, educators became aware of just how monocultural traditional curricular content was. To rectify this, they often found single stories from other cultures to address the inequity. Now, in the second decade of the 21st century, teachers are aware of the danger of any single story representing any group.

This strategy helps you discover how many stories your curriculum tells and whose stories they are. It also helps you think about whose stories are missing and may need to be included.

NOTE TO INSTRUCTOR

Model this strategy for students with a sample unit from a curriculum of your choosing. Provide students with a unit/section from a curriculum guide from their content area, or ask students to bring a sample unit from their field observation schools for this strategy.

STEP-BY-STEP INSTRUCTIONS

Pairs analyze a curriculum sample using these questions:

1. What particular groups or stories are named in the curriculum? If none are named, what categories or spaces exist in which teachers must provide specific examples?

2. What materials or resources are provided? Whose stories do they include?

3. How are the stories told? Is the point of view idealized, simplistic, realistic?

4. To what extent are students recognized as resources? In what ways?

5. How much teacher choice or control is there in determining which stories to tell?

6. Whole-group discussion.

LOOKING BACK/LOOKING AHEAD

Write about your experience with this strategy. What surprised you? What did you learn?

_____

_____

_____

_____

_____

Your Turn

Lesson Planning

RATIONALE

Strategies 33 through 37 ask you to analyze currently accepted best practice strategies. In this strategy, you will incorporate these types of culturally responsive strategies with content from your own subject areas (e.g., science, math, English, history) to create a lesson plan.

NOTE TO INSTRUCTOR

We have included a Sample Lesson Plan. You may want to tailor our headings to match your University's lesson plan template. We have also included a template for writing a unit plan (Strategy 40). You may want to download a sample unit plan from the companion website (**http://www.sagepub.com/buckelew**) to share with your students.

SAMPLE LESSON PLAN

Date:

Name:

Subject: English/Humanities

Time Frame: Two 48- to 52-minute class periods

Grade Level/s: Tenth Grade

Lesson Topic/Title: Friendship

Where does this lesson fit into the unit? Pre-reading/anticipatory set for a thematic unit on "Friendship, Loyalty, and Leadership," which includes *Julius Caesar* by William Shakespeare.

Materials: Notebooks, 3 × 5 cards

Lesson Plan Goal/s: To give students the opportunity to make authentic connections to Shakespeare's play *Julius Caesar* and one of its themes—friendship.

Objectives:

1. Students will be able to share and analyze the attributes of a friend.

2. Students will be able to understand many of the issues that they will read about in *Julius Caesar* and subsequent readings.

3. Students will be able to make connections between the theme of friendship in *Julius Caesar* and their own lives.

STATE STANDARDS

Pedagogy: How are you going to accomplish your goal/s and objectives?

Anticipatory Set:

1. Focused freewrite: Write about a best friend. Why do you consider this person to be a best friend?

2. Students pair-share their focused freewrites.

3. Invite volunteers to share their focused freewrites with the whole class.

4. List attributes of a friend based on group discussion.

Modeling/Demonstration/Explanation: Explain to students that one of the themes in the play, *Julius Caesar*, is friendship. Friendship appears to be timeless.

Activities:
Day 1

1. Break class into committees of 4–5 students. Use color-coded Shakespeare cards to place students in committees.

2. Each committee lists 5 qualities that qualify a person as a friend.

3. Each committee lists 5 problems that could cause the possible dissolution of a friendship.

4. Teacher: Explain/share example of a constitution.

5. When groups are finished listing the qualities and problems, ask each group to draft a Friendship Constitution integrating the ideas from the group. Students should include 8–10 traits and 4–8 infractions in their Friendship Constitutions.

6. Students may choose to illustrate their constitution.

Day 2

Materials: Student drafts of Friendship Constitutions, 3 × 5 cards

Activities:

1. Each group selects a tribune who will represent their group in the senate and read their Friendship Constitution to class.

2. The tribunes read their Friendship Constitutions to the class. Students may need to read each constitution more than once.

3. The class votes on which constitution they think is best.

4. If there is a tie, the opposing tribunes will need to argue for their respective Friendship Constitutions.

5. The entire populace will then vote again based on the debate.

6. Once the class Friendship Constitution is decided upon, students do a quick, focused freewrite regarding their reaction to the overall task.

7. Questions/topics they might address in their focused freewrite: Relationship of activity to the play they are about to read. What are they wondering? Did they find the activity meaningful? Why? Were there surprises? Can they draw any conclusions about coming to a consensus in a large group? These questions can lead into more specific questions regarding the play.

8. For the discussion that follows, here are questions you might add to the above list: What is the role of personal friendships in creating a group governing structure? How easy is it to maintain friendships when one holds a position of power?

Checking for Understanding—Exit Slip: An "exit slip" is a formative assessment that can be used to assess student learning. The exit slip asks students to describe, explain, or analyze their experience with the day's learning. For example, ask students to write three to five sentences in which they describe what they learned or what they need to learn in order to fully understand the day's lesson.

Accommodations/Differentiated Instruction: Students can be given the option of designing a visual representation of the Friendship Constitution. Students might also create skits to illustrate the qualities of friendship and to illustrate the infractions.

Extensions: During reading, return to the Friendship Constitution. Ask students how the characters live up to the class criteria for friendship. How often do they fail? Create a Friendship or Mediation Task Force that will help to arbitrate or mediate on issues that arise between friends. Students might participate in mediation training to become part of the task force, which will help to resolve classroom conflicts.

Research Topic: Students might choose to interview someone in a position of power/leadership regarding the role of friendship in relation to power/leadership.

Theoretical Base: Write a few sentences citing the theory or theories that inform your lesson. This lesson includes elements of the constructivist theory, which supports learning as social and collaborative. In addition, the suggestions for differentiated instruction address Howard Gardner's theory of multiple intelligences and the classroom as ecosystem in which students work individually as well as collaborate.

Teacher Reflection (to be completed after the lesson): What went well? Why? What would you do differently? Why?

Your Turn

Collaborative Unit Planning

Strategy 40

The unit plan template is designed so that you can collaborate with members of your class to design a unit based on your content area. The template provides guidelines for creating a culturally responsive unit plan. You will incorporate culturally responsive strategies with content from your own content areas (e.g., science, math, English, history) to create a unit plan.

NOTE TO INSTRUCTOR

The following template is designed for groups of students. We find that groups of three to four work best. The template can also be given as an individual assignment. Whichever approach works best for you, we suggest providing in-class time for planning so that students can consult with you and each other.

UNIT PLAN GUIDELINES

I. Cover: (Title of Unit, your name/s, date, course and meeting time, and instructor name)

II. Title Page:

- Title of unit
- Themes/Essential Questions
- Grade level
- Time/Scope and Sequence (minimum: 3 weeks)

III. Table of Contents

IV. General Introduction/Rationale

V. Topics to consider in your Rationale:

Purpose: What is the purpose for this unit? Is it required by the curriculum? Is it something students have expressed interest in? Is it relevant to your students' lives outside of the classroom?

Concepts: What are the important concepts, the big understandings, that you want students to develop and learn?

Context: How does it fit into the rest of the year? What are possible connections to other units? Other courses (cross-curricular)?

Length: 1 to 2 double-spaced pages

VI. Calendar: The calendar should indicate highlights of daily activities; i.e., include those activities that you would normally write up as full-fledged lessons.

VII. Introduction—Springboard/Anticipatory Lesson: This lesson should introduce the unit.

VIII. Two lessons per group member; i.e., each group member will write two lessons for the unit. These lessons should be integral to your unit, but they do not have to be consecutive. Make sure connections to state standards/theories are clear (see sample lesson in Strategy 39).

IX. Rubrics/Assessments/Tests for each lesson: These may be included within each lesson (formal/informal/formative/summative).

X. Culminating Activity: Some sort of celebration/publication/demonstration of learning. You may write a paragraph description or lesson plan for the culminating activity. Indicate number of days/time allotted for the preparation and presentation.

Standards: Each lesson should include a paragraph or bullets connecting the activities in the lesson to the state standards.

Theorists/Theories: Each lesson should include a few sentences that make connections between the activities/content and one or more theorists/theories.

References and Suggested Readings

Alvine, L., & Cullum, L. (Eds.). (1999). *Breaking the cycle: Gender, literacy, and learning.* Portsmouth, NH: Boynton/Cook.

Anzaldúa, G. (1999). *Borderlands/La frontera: The new mestiza* (2nd ed.). San Francisco: Aunt Lute Books.

Applebee, A. (1996). *Curriculum as conversation: Transforming traditions of teaching and learning.* Chicago: University of Chicago Press.

Atwell, N. (1998). *In the middle: New understanding about writing, reading, and learning* (2nd ed.). Portsmouth, NH: Heinemann.

Banks, J. (1988). Approaches to multicultural curriculum reform. *Multicultural Leader, 1*(2), 1–3.

Baxter, P., & Jack, S. (2008). Qualitative case study methodology: Study design and implementation for novice researchers. *The Qualitative Report, 13*(4), 544–559.

Beers, K., Probst, R., & Rief, L. (2007). *Adolescent literacy: Turning promise into practice.* Portsmouth, NH: Heinemann.

Belli, G. (1992). *Rediscovering America/Redescubriendo America.* Washington, DC: Teaching for Change.

Benard, B. (1991). The foundations of the resiliency framework: From research to practice. In N. Henderson (Ed.), *Resiliency in action.* Retrieved June 16, 2010, from http://www.resiliency.com/htm/research.htm.

Benard, B. (2004). *Resiliency: What we have learned.* San Francisco: WestEd.

Bentley, A. F. (1954). The fiction of retinal image. In S. Ratner (Ed.), *Inquiry into inquiries* (p. 285). Boston: Beacon Press.

Blakesley, D. (1992). He/man and the masters of discourse. In N. McCracken & B. Appleby,

Gender issues in the teaching of English (pp. 23–38). Portsmouth, NH: Boynton/Cook.

Britcher, T. (2009). Motivation through preferred activities. *Reader Teacher, 102*(2), 72–77.

Brown, J. (1994). *How to write a rationale.* Adapted from SLATE Starter Sheet, National Council of Teachers of English (NCTE), April 1994. Retrieved June 27, 2010, from http://www.ncte.org/library/NCTEFiles/Involved/Action/Rationale_HowtoWrite.pdf.

Buckelew, M. B. (2003). The value of art in the English classroom: Imagination, making the tacit visible. *English Journal, 92*(5) 49–55.

Buckelew, M. B. (2009). First steps for reaching and teaching diverse populations: The classroom ecosystem and transactional literary theory. *International Journal of Learning, 16*(2), 43–54.

Cisneros, S. (1991). *The house on Mango Street.* New York: Vintage.

Coles, R. (1986). *The moral life of children.* New York: Houghton Mifflin.

Delpit, L. (1995). *Other people's children: Cultural conflict in the classroom.* New York: Norton.

Delpit, L. (2008). *The skin that we speak: Thoughts on language and culture in the classroom.* New York: The New Press.

Dong, Y. R. (2004). Don't keep them in the dark! Teaching metaphors to English language learners. *English Journal, 93*(4), 29–35.

Eggen, P., & Kauchak, D. (2006). *Educational psychology: Windows on classrooms* (7th ed.). Upper Saddle River, NJ: Prentice Hall.

Fishman, A. (1988). *Amish literacy: What and how it means.* Portsmouth, NH: Heinemann.

Fishman, A. (1990). Becoming literate: A lesson from the Amish. In A. Lunsford, H. Moglen,

& J. Slevin (Eds.), *The right to literacy* (pp. 29–38). New York: Modern Language Association.

Fishman, A. (1995). Finding ways in: Redefining multicultural literature. *English Journal, 84*(6), 73–79.

Freire, P. (1993). *Pedagogy of the oppressed* (20th anniv. ed.). New York: Continuum. Retrieved June 21, 2010, from http://www.webster.edu/~corbetre/philosophy/education/freire/freire-2.html.

Freire, P. (2008). The "banking" concept of education. In D. Bartholomae & A. Petrosky (Eds.), *Ways of reading: An anthology for writers* (8th ed., pp. 242–258). Boston: Bedford/St. Martin's.

Gay, G. (2000). *Culturally responsive teaching: Theory, research, and practice.* New York: Teachers College Press.

Geertz, C. (1973). *The interpretation of cultures.* New York: Basic Books.

Glynn, S. M. (2008). Making science concepts meaningful to students: Teaching with analogies. In S. Mikelskis-Seifert, U. Ringelband, & M. Brückmann (Eds.), *Four decades of research in science education: From curriculum development to quality improvement* (pp. 113–125). Münster, Germany: Waxmann.

Gollnick, D. M., & Chinn, P. C. (2006). *Multicultural education in a pluralistic society* (8th ed.). Boston: Allyn & Bacon.

Graves, D. (1975). The child, the writing process, and the role of the professional. In W. Petty & P. J. Price (Eds.), *The writing processes of students.* Buffalo: State University of New York.

Graves, D. (2006). *A sea of faces: The importance of getting to know your students.* Portsmouth, NH: Heinemann.

Harste, J. C., & Leland, C. (1999). Testing the water with mini-inquiry projects. In R. S. Hubbard, & B. M. Power (Eds.), *Living the questions: A guide for teacher-researchers* (pp. 68–69). Portsmouth, NH: Heinemann.

Harvey, S., & Daniels, H. (2009). *Comprehension and collaboration: Inquiry circles in action.* Portsmouth, NH: Heinemann.

Heath, S. B. (1983). *Ways with words: Language, life, and work in communities and classrooms.* Cambridge, UK: Cambridge University Press.

Hubbard, R. S., & Power, B. M. (1999). *Living the questions: A guide for teacher-researchers.* Portsmouth, NH: Heinemann.

Hubbard, R. S., & Power, B. M. (2003). *The art of classroom inquiry: A handbook for teacher-researchers* (Rev. ed.). Portsmouth, NH: Heinemann.

Jalajas, D., & Sutton, R. (1984). Feuds in student groups: Coping with whiners, martyrs, saboteurs, bullies, and deadbeats. *Journal of Management Education, 9*(4), 94–102.

Johnston, P. (2004). *Choice words: How our language affects children's learning.* Portland, ME: Stenhouse Publishers.

Kaplan, J., & Bernays, A. (1999). *The language of names: What we call ourselves and why it matters.* New York: Simon & Schuster.

Kincaid, J. (1991). Girl. In S. Barnett (Ed.), *The Harper anthology of fiction* (1991–1190). New York: HarperCollins.

King-Shaver, B., & Hunter, A. (2009). *Adolescent literacy and differentiated instruction.* Portsmouth, NH: Heinemann.

Kohl, H. (1994). *"I won't learn from you" and other thoughts on creative maladjustment.* New York: Norton.

Lyon, G. E. (1999). *Where I'm from: Where poems come from.* Spring, TX: Absey & Co.

Mayher, J. (1990). *Uncommon sense: Theoretical practice in language education.* Portsmouth, NH: Boynton/Cook.

McCann, T., Johannessen, L., Kahn, E., & Smagorinsky, P. (2005). *Reflective teaching, reflective learning: How to develop critically engaged readers, writers, and speakers.* Portsmouth, NH: Heinemann.

McCracken, N. M., & Appleby, B. C. (Eds.). (1992). *Gender issues in the teaching of English.* Portsmouth, NH: Boynton/Cook.

Meece, J. (2006). Gender and motivation. *Journal of School Psychology, 44*(5), 351–373.

Miller, D. (2008). *Teaching with intention: Defining beliefs, aligning practices, taking action.* Portland, ME: Stenhouse Publishers.

McIntosh, P. (1989, July/August). White privilege: Unpacking the invisible knapsack. *Peace and Freedom Magazine,* 10–12.

National Association for Multicultural Education. (2003, February). *Resolutions & position papers: Multicultural education.* Bethesda, MD: Author. Retrieved June 27, 2010, from http://nameorg.org/papers.

Newkirk, T. (2009). *Holding on to good ideas in a time of bad ones: Six literacy principles worth fighting for.* Portsmouth, NH: Heinemann.

O'Brien, T. (1998). *The things they carried.* New York: Broadway.

Ponterotto, J. (2006). Brief note on the origins, evolution, and meaning of the qualitative research concept "thick description." *The Qualitative Report, 11*(3), 538–549. Available at http://www.nova.edu/ssss/QR/QR11-3/ponterotto.pdf.

Pugh, S. L., Hicks, J. W., & Davis, M. (1997). *Metaphorical ways of knowing: The imaginative nature of thought and expression.* Urbana, IL: National Council of Teachers of English.

Putz, M. (2006). *A teacher's guide to the multigenre research project.* Portsmouth, NH: Heinemann.

Quate, S., & McDermott, J. (2009). *Clock watchers: Six steps to motivating and engaging disengaged students across content areas.* Portsmouth, NH: Heinemann.

Romano, T. (2000). *Blending genre, altering style: Writing the multigenre paper.* Portsmouth, NH: Boynton/Cook.

Schaafsma, D. (1993). *Eating on the street: Teaching literacy in a multicultural society.* Pittsburgh, PA: University of Pittsburgh Press.

Shearer, B. (2000). A student-directed written inquiry. In M. E. Vogt & M. McLaughlin (Eds.), *Creativity and innovation in content area teaching* (pp. 209–229). New York: Christopher-Gordon Publishers.

Spender, D. (1990). *Man made language* (2nd ed.). London: Routledge.

Steele, C. (2003). Stereotype threat and African-American student achievement. In T. Perry, C. Steele, & A. Hillard, III, *Young, gifted, and black: Promoting high achievement among African-American students* (pp. 109–130). Boston: Beacon Press.

Strickland, J. (2004). Just the FAQs: An alternative to teaching the research paper. *English Journal, 94*(1), 23–28.

Tatum, B. D. (2003). *Why are all the black kids sitting together in the cafeteria? A psychologist explains the development of racial identity.* New York: Basic Books.

Tatum, B. D. (2008). *Can we talk about race? And other conversations in an era of resegregation.* Boston: Beacon Press.

Wanner, S. (1994.) *On with the story: Adolescents learning through narrative.* Portsmouth, NH:Boynton/Cook.

Wheatley, M. (2005). *Finding our way: Leadership for an uncertain time.* San Francisco: Berrett-Koehler.

Wheeler, R., & Swords, R. (2006). *Code-switching: Teaching Standard English in urban classrooms.* Urbana, IL: National Council of Teachers of English.

Yamato, G. (2004). Something about the subject makes it hard to name. In M. L. Andersen & P. H. Collins (Eds.), *Race, Class, and Gender* (5th ed., pp. 99–108). New York: Thomson/Wadsworth.

About the Authors

Mary Bellucci Buckelew and **Andrea Fishman** are professors of English and English Education at West Chester University in West Chester, PA, where they direct the PA Writing and Literature Project, a National Writing Project site devoted to the improvement of writing and reading instruction across the grades and across the curriculum. They are codevelopers of site-specific programs that help schools close their achievement gaps, whatever the parameters in a given setting. Mary and Andrea have a combined 36 years of experience as English teachers in middle and high school classrooms in Pennsylvania, New Jersey, and New Mexico.

Andrea is the author of the book *Amish Literacy: What and How It Means*. Both she and Mary have published numerous articles in peer-reviewed journals including *Language Arts, English Journal, Voices From the Middle, English Education, Kappan, Educational Leadership,* and *The International Journal of Learning*. Mary and Andrea are frequent presenters at national and international conferences.

Supporting researchers for more than 40 years

Research methods have always been at the core of SAGE's publishing program. Founder Sara Miller McCune published SAGE's first methods book, *Public Policy Evaluation*, in 1970. Soon after, she launched the *Quantitative Applications in the Social Sciences* series—affectionately known as the "little green books."

Always at the forefront of developing and supporting new approaches in methods, SAGE published early groundbreaking texts and journals in the fields of qualitative methods and evaluation.

Today, more than 40 years and two million little green books later, SAGE continues to push the boundaries with a growing list of more than 1,200 research methods books, journals, and reference works across the social, behavioral, and health sciences. Its imprints—Pine Forge Press, home of innovative textbooks in sociology, and Corwin, publisher of PreK–12 resources for teachers and administrators—broaden SAGE's range of offerings in methods. SAGE further extended its impact in 2008 when it acquired CQ Press and its best-selling and highly respected political science research methods list.

From qualitative, quantitative, and mixed methods to evaluation, SAGE is the essential resource for academics and practitioners looking for the latest methods by leading scholars.

For more information, visit **www.sagepub.com**.